SAVAGE CIRCLE

Mick N. Baker

Copyright 2023 Michael Baker

The moral right of the author has been asserted.

Some characters and events in this publication are based on real people and

events… And some aren't.

All rights reserved.

No part of this publication may be reproduced, stored in a retrieval system, or transmitted on any form or by any means, without the prior permission in writing of the author, nor be otherwise circulated in any form of binding or cover other than in which it is published and without a similar condition including this condition being imposed on the subsequent purchase.

To Chris, Jess and Abbie

For Mum and Dad

Savage Circle

Cheers to everyone who bought The Cxnterbury Tales.

Savage Circle

Chapter One - Down on The Farm

Chapter Two - Cabbages

Chapter Three - The Harvest

Chapter Four - Friends, Romans, Countrymen

Chapter Five - Cheech and Chong

Chapter Six - Threesome's a Crowd

Chapter Seven - Dirty Den Gets Clean

Chapter Eight - Dog Days

Chapter Nine - Relics

Chapter Ten - Charles Dickens Machete Attack

Chapter Eleven - 'Boots Scum Here We Come'

Chapter Twelve - Paranoid John Loses Control

Chapter Thirteen - Savage Circle

Chapter Fourteen - No Sleep 'til Hertford

'It was the best of times, it was the worst of times.'

Charles Dickens.

'The game of life is hard to play,
You're going to lose it anyway'

Johnny Mandel / Michael Altman.

'Life's a Savage Circle'

Owen, Jennings, Fox, Ruffy.

Edited by Abbie Baker

Dedicated to Felix Michael Keeble

Chapter One

Down on The Farm

Sele Farm Estate in Hertford had a bad reputation, even for a satellite estate.

It was no wonder. Stampy's family had come and gone as had the Duggens. I didn't know why Stampy's family had gone, but I certainly knew where they had moved to. As for the Duggens, well, I knew all about that. Knew too much. Sometimes I even dreamt about it. That was never going to go away.

Irene Duggen had decided enough was enough after her youngest, Little Dugs, had died after the fight on the Berecroft estate in Harlow. Little Dugs had fought hard to stay alive - his body steadfast - but Kipper's baseball bat had mashed his brain into a pulp. Six weeks of prayers, pleading, begging to a god unknown had come to nothing. On a cold rainy Friday night at exactly the same time that Irene had seen Little Dug's broken shell of a body for the first time in Princess Alexandra Hospital, she watched, devastated, as the duty doctor switched off his life support machine and as the lights around him blinked out, he died.

Danny and me still didn't know how to feel about it all. On one side a kid about the same age as Danny's sister, Tara, had died. On the other, the little cunt would have showed us no mercy - he would have kicked the shit out of us, as he did with many others when the odds were stacked in his favour. He probably would've laughed hearing we were being kept alive by a machine, being force-fed and shitting in a bag. One thing we did know was, we could never tell anyone about it.

Whiff had his suspicions, as did Mark Harper, the twat who instigated the whole thing with his promise of local sensi, but I knew if I told anyone, even a close mate, then we were vulnerable. If word got out, the repercussions would be devastating, not only for Danny and me but for our families too, even if the Duggens had moved to Marsh Farm in Luton. It would only take the remaining two brothers half an hour to get to us. I did worry about Danny though; sometimes, it was like he would only do things so he could tell people about it. He loved a story, loved watching the people around him gape at the crazy antics he got up to, but in this case, he stayed quiet and kept it to himself. I thought it was amazing how the prospect of a good kicking could stiffen up the loosest of tongues.

I had moved to 'the Farm' after my mum and dad had gone to live in Cornwall, into a nice big airy west-facing bedroom in a flat on Longwood Road with the main tenants Pete Owen and his girlfriend Janine Badwick.

Pete was a decent bloke, liked his music, was into The Clash, Siouxsie and the Banshees and a new up-and-coming band called The Smiths. Janine Badwick, however, was a right stuck-up cow. It was loath at first sight for her; I could see it even before I'd opened my mouth. Luckily, when I did open my mouth, in amongst me and Pete's chat about bands, I happened to mention that I had played a CND benefit. Pete, missing the daggers being thrown at him by his girlfriend, had shaken my hand on the spot, telling me I could move in any time I wanted.

On move-in day, Pete was at university, so it was down to Janine to settle the new tenant in. I knocked on the bright blue door, waited, knocked again, waited. Eventually, begrudgingly, with a look on her face like I was some Gypsy wanting to sell her pegs at the door while my accomplice was sneaking in her backdoor to steal her VHS, she edged the door open. I wasn't sure she was going to let me at first, then some kind of reason must have come over her, and she made way for... For lord knows what.

Janine pointed her long bony finger upstairs in the direction of my room and vanished into the kitchen, closing the door behind her. I couldn't believe how angry she was; she was absolutely seething. Even later on, after I had got my meagre stash of possessions in, even when I gave her the deposit and first month's rent of £200, she barely cracked a smile. I had seen it all before, though. It was no big deal. No problem at all. This was a new place to live, so I wouldn't be seeing much of Badwitch (as I started calling her) anyway. I wanted to get out and about -see what was going on. See if the Farm lived up to its reputation.

On the Ridgeway, the main road running across the estate, it had been a pretty frosty reception too, with a few people dossing out the newcomer, especially as I had moved into the so-called 'posh area.' This was essentially the council flats in Longwood Road that had been sold off in Thatcher's house fire sale. I knew posh, and Longwood Road wasn't it. Nowhere near it. The blocks were built in exactly the same way as all the other blocks on the estate. Sixteen two-bedroom flats, eight on the ground level, eight above them. All layered in pebble-dashed concrete.

People soon warmed to me though.

Once I'd got myself out and about, it wasn't long before I bumped into a few familiar faces. Dirty Den was the first of many; he had moved in when his missus had kicked him out again. It was 'final this time,' so he told me, and it had all been over a box of Swan Vesta matches.

Rosie had gone to do some cleaning work, to give them a bit of extra money, telling Den to pick the kids up after school. 'It couldn't have been simpler' he told me. He settled in to watch TVAM when suddenly he had an impulse for a can of chicken soup. He joked that, after going cold turkey the first time and living on the stuff, he had become 'addicted to it.' He nipped into the kitchen, grabbed up a can from the stack, opened it, then panned it. Then when he came to light the gas ring, there were no matches about. He looked high and low, pulling out draws, poking around in cupboards, cursing the stupid woman: 'Where the fucking hell are the matches for the gas, I always leave them by the cooker 'cause they're the cooker matches.' Suddenly a memory popped up in his head; there was a box of Swan Vestas up in his sock drawer in the bedroom. Den told me he was 'smiling,' thinking his head 'isn't as fucked up as people said it was.' He ambled upstairs into the bedroom, opened the draw and 'low and behold,' there they were. Back downstairs in the kitchen, he swivelled the knob on the cooker, heard the hiss of the gas, opened the box of matches and there inside was a 'nice wrap of brown.'

'He couldn't believe his luck; he couldn't believe how little methadone he was getting in his script these days either'. He popped the pan of soup onto the ring and hastily made his way to get his 'toolbox'. He thought 'I'll have a little bit of this, then a bit of soup and settle back and watch the rest of TVAM – hopefully, I'll miss that fucking twat, Roland Rat.'

A few hours later, he woke up to find Rosie standing over him 'screaming blue murder' in his face. She was really going at him: 'bastard, cunt, shit, fuck, wanker, asshole' - disgorged from her 'heavenly distorted face moulded into the ceiling above him'. Once he'd managed to get his senses back, which wasn't long with 'Rosie giving me hell like that,' he saw the windows were wide open, then he smelt gas: 'A fucking lot of it.' Rosie had kicked him out the next day and he had moved his few possessions to Aiden's place on the Farm.

Bunny Hills was the next familiar face I bumped into, well, I say familiar face. He was unrecognisable from the kid at Richard Hole School that I had threatened.

I was wandering along the Ridgeway when I saw an old tramp being pulled along by a group of dogs; he must have had about ten dogs. As he got closer, I looked down and found something interesting to look at on the path, then as he passed, I heard a friendly 'Skinner!!?'

I stopped and looked up, thinking, who the fucking hell is this weirdo, and through a mass of rats' tail-like hair, Bunny Hills's eyes gleamed back at me.

"Thought that was you, what you doing up here?" he grinned.

Bunny stood back as I told him my story, while the dogs closed in around us. I made it as short as possible because I had my own questions to ask. Like, what the fuck is going on with all these dogs?

Bunny scratched ferociously at his scalp, grinned through his matted beard, scratched again, and told that me this was his 'Zoo' and 'They were a lifesaver in the cold winter months.' He had been squatting on the Farm for three years. It was easy to start with, he'd find an empty flat, break in, put a magnet on the electricity meter, and sit back and enjoy the free tenancy. It would take the council ages to work out what was going on - usually a couple of months – then, once they did, they couldn't turn off the electricity in the squat without blacking out the entire block.

Bunny and me cracked up laughing, it was fucking ludicrous, the stupid wankers. Then, his face clouded over like a pub garden in summertime.

He told me that last winter they sorted out their problem, isolated the supply of the squats and hit the switch, turning off his free electricity and leaving him with no light, no heat, nothing. The winter was freezing. That was when he had the idea of collecting dogs. They would not only warn him of the impending raid by the bailiffs, but he could also sleep with them at night to keep himself warm.

I felt one of them nuzzling me. Looking down, I saw a big-eyed brown greyhound on the end of its string, gazing up at me lovingly.

"Oh, he likes you, doesn't he?" said Bunny, smiling broadly, picking errantly at his Mato Grosso beard.

I nodded, patting the little fella on the head. "Ha, yeah, what's his name?"

Bunny grinned. "Dog Friday. And that's Monday, Tuesday, Wednesday, Thursday, Sunday, Saturday," he told me, as they checked my scent, pulling on their individual strings.

"Hold up, there's eight of them, who's the other one, Clint Eastwood, the Dog with no name?"

"Nah, that one, the little one, that's Stinky Terrier, that's Bashers' dog. I'm taking care of him while Basher's in Feltham."

Not surprised, nodding my head like it was old news, I said, "Go on then, what happened to Bash this time?"

Bunny cracked up.

I thought this is going to be good.

Basher had broken into Tarling's Hardware store in Ware on a mission to get some glue. He loved his glue did Bash. The trouble was that all the shops around Hertford and Ware knew it too, they wouldn't sell him any. So desperate for a bag one night, he'd kicked Tarling's back door in and found himself in a glue sniffers paradise.

Tins and tins of contact adhesive, impact adhesive, grab adhesive, grip adhesive surrounded him. There was every type he could imagine. He couldn't contain himself, so he had a quick bag there and then.

Bash had told him, 'I zoned out, dreaming of little Hitlers coming down on Swastika parachutes falling out the sky.'

A few minutes later when the flying dictators had disappeared, so did Bash, taking enough glue to not only sink The Titanic but to build it too.

I creased up laughing at the thought of Basher high tailing it down Ware High Street with towers of Evo tins in his arms.

"So how did he end up in Feltham?"

Bunny held my eye for a moment, waiting for the joke to ferment before revealing, "When the old bill showed up the next day, they found his Giro, with his name and address on it glued to the wall!!!"

"Fuck off, you're joking man?"

"No, straight up. He said he'd put it in his back pocket earlier on and forgot to cash it. It must have dropped out when he was spaced out."

I cracked up, thinking of Bash's Giro stuck on the wall, I bet the old bill couldn't believe their luck. It was only a matter of time though, Bash was –

Suddenly pandemonium broke out in the pack of dogs. Stinky Terrier, leading the assault, snarled, ripped forward, stretching his green string to breaking point. Turning, I saw a short thick-set, black-haired punk shouldering up towards us.

"For fuck's sake Hillsey, keep your duvet under control will you," said the short spikey-haired punk.

"Sorry Renny, it's Stinky Terrier, he can be a right vicious bastard. Clam up will you Stink," he said, pulling the slavering beast back, with one hand, while scratching at his crotch with the other. "Where you off to then?" he continued, dogs and bollocks calmed for now.

"I've got the Bewildered, Bestial Cowlick and Jam Rag Jury at the Square tonight," said Renny, keeping his eye on the nasty little terrier.

"Oh nice, Skinner's in a band, aren't you?"

I nodded back in the affirmative. "Yeah, er, we…"

"Yeah, I saw them playing at Bowes with the Destructors and the Subhumans," said Renny before I could find the words. "Good, aren't they?"

"They were OK, they sounded like a lot of other bands," he told us.

I nodded my head, appreciating his honesty. "Yeah, well, we've moved on now, hopefully," I said, hopefully.

Renny pulled a smile and put his hand out. "Tell me when your next gig is Skinner and I'll be there."

"OK… Renny?" I said, giving his hand a firm, friendly, shake.

Renny, Hillsey and me stood chatting, passing the time of day for a while, then with the dogs straining at their strings for some proper exercise, we said our goodbyes and I watched them walk away.

With the dogs out in front of them, they looked like they were being pulled along on an invisible sleigh. I nodded, feeling good about meeting some new people. Hillsey shouted back that I 'should go round Lenny the Lamp's place on the Ridgeway.' He told me, 'I'm there most nights, me and the zoo have got our own room.' Waving back, grinning at the Ridgeway's husky handlers, I thought, yeah, that could be a laugh.

***

A few days later, after bumping into Renny, who was on his way to Lenny's place with a bag of bits and pieces he needed to ditch, he invited me to tag along. I said yeah, and fell into step with him.

Renny and me strolled along Tudor Way, then onto the Ridgeway, taking in the air, enjoying the vibe of living in a close-knit community, chatting away as we went. He was a funny little bloke, he must have only been about 5.8, but what he lacked in height, he made up with his lust for life. He lived for his music, punk, and metal, but didn't have one record to his name. He was into gigs. That's the only way he was interested in listening to music: live, beer in hand, ear against the speaker. I was surprised he could hear at all; he should have been completely mutton Jeff.

He would travel anywhere to see a band, using any means necessary to get there: 'trainers, trains or automobiles.' He'd get there early too for the support bands – all of them. He'd watch anyone. He knew everything about every obscure band you couldn't think of and didn't know. Vocalists, guitarists, bass players, drummers. Who was in this band, who used to be in that band. If he could've gotten onto mastermind with the specialist subject 'Bands that nobody has heard of and their members and replacement members', he'd have won that poxy glass bowl, no problem.

Renny leant hard on Lenny's half-boarded-up door, and bit by bit it slowly gave, finally juddering open. Renny gave me a wink, snorted, and we wandered into the kitchen. Fucking hell, I thought, maybe I do live in the posh part after all. Bomb damage was how I would have described it. It was like Taz the Tasmanian devil had been the housekeeper for, well, forever. If Mary Poppins showed up, she would have chucked the filthy towel in and hung herself up from the single stained light bulb hanging in the middle of the room. Reverend Hilary Charman's house back in Thundridge was bad, but this place made it look all cleanliness and light.

A nice-looking middle-aged woman greeted us with a cheery 'hello' from the hallway on the opposite side of the kitchen. I peered over the detritus on what was left of the kitchen table... I couldn't believe my eyes. It wasn't, was it? It fucking well was. It was Kipper's girlfriend from the Berecroft estate in Harlow. Her beaming eyes passed over Renny, then came to an abrupt halt on me.

A moment of recognition? I thought there must be. I waited for that moment, then with a minute shake of her head, she offered us a cup of tea and we both nodded back in unison. While I took in the room, Renny and Trace - as I heard Renny call her - chatted away, discussing the contents of his bag: Bottles of Blue Stratos and Brut Aftershave freshly nicked from Boots the thief's paradise in Ware.

Mould-encrusted pots and pans filled the sink and were strewn across the draining board and onto the worktops. On the kitchen table lay a motorbike tyre with a carving knife rammed into it. There was a smell of shit about the place too. Freshly laid shit. I felt a nudge and Renny handed me a steaming hot cup of tea, saying 'bottoms up' with a wry smile on his face. 'Cheers,' I said to Trace. She nodded, didn't give me a second look, and we followed her through the hallway into the sitting room at the back of the flat.

Now it was my turn to baulk. Sitting on the settee with a couple of other blokes and a girl sat Robbo 'The Bank' Barker. He'd been sniffing around Cerys after our Ware College gig. She'd told me her and her mate Caroline had had a couple of drinks with him and his brother Mike in The Punch House, or The Get Punched Up House as we called it, the casuals pub in Ware, and he'd followed her into the ladies' toilet asking her for a blow job. She'd told him to 'fuck off' with so much venom that he'd backtracked. Opening his arms innocently, he told her he 'was only joking', 'it was nothing', but in that moment Cerys had felt vulnerable - there was no one else about. He was a big bloke, six foot four and strong from the building sites. It had really shit her up. So once 'the perv bastard' had disappeared into the men's, she legged it back into the main bar to Caroline, grabbed her confused mate by the arm and sneaked out the pub through the back door.

Robbo gave me a cursory nod; he didn't have a clue who I was either. He said a sly 'alright' to Renny who gave him a big grin and carried on chatting with the others. I snorted, and after moving a mouldy old copy of 'What Bike' off another settee opposite Robbo, we took a pew.

I sat listening to the conversation, took a sip of my tea and noticed there was a pea floating around in it. Renny gave me a nudge, whispering, "Get it down yer, it all goes to make a turd."

I shook my head, getting back to the conversation. If I was going live here for any amount of time, which I wanted to, I was going to have to learn and learn quickly. This wasn't leafy, idyllic Thundridge living under Maddy and Dummy's roof. I was on my own now. I would sink or swim, and knowledge could be the difference. Knowing who was who was definitely the right place to start.

Jason Brown, another Farm dweller around the same age as me, was the topic of conversation. I had heard about him before. He was a weightlifter, broad-shouldered and muscular with a penchant for young girls. He had been seen time and time again, chatting with second-year girls at the shops at the top of Tudor Way. He might have been a big bloke, the sort of bloke, you would have thought the girls would go for, but rumour had it he was still a virgin. Jason Brown had tried it on with most of the girls around the estate; even the old boiler who worked in the chip shop next to the shops had said no when he had asked her on a date.

A few other names got thrown about: Tank, Pat Cotis, Paranoid John, Hippy John, Nicky Kuczek, Viv Marshall; all people I knew from the Manpower Services and Herts Archaeological Unit. I'd been working with them since before I'd left home. They were a decent bunch of people, and more importantly, they were a fucking good laugh. Enjoying the vibe as the stories came and went, I lifted the teacup to mouth, suddenly remembered the pea, then deftly placed it into a Cornflakes box down at the side of the settee. It was then I noticed there were a couple of toddlers playing behind it.

One had a beer can in its hand, pressing it down onto a piece of newspaper while the other one carefully drew around it. The one with the pen, a girl I think - I wasn't too sure as they both had matted long blonde hair - looked up at me, gave me a tomato ketchup smile, then got back to drawing. Beaming back at them, I gave them a little wave.

Trace said, "Hope you two are behaving yourselves around there," gently chiding them, and they both answered with a cheery, 'yes'.

Trace took a deep breath. "I went to visit Kipper yesterday."

Slowly twisting back in my seat, I was all ears now; maybe she did know who I was after all, maybe I was in trouble, big fucking trouble. Robbo and the other two, Shads and Brandon, were big blokes and from what I had seen, all of them liked Trace. They'd have busted my fucking head if I had upset her. When was this bullshit going to end? I thought. Was it ever going to end?

Trace continued, her eyes welling up. She had been 'up The Scrubs to see him after his sentence for GBH had been upped to manslaughter' and he had told her, 'Get on with your life, don't wait for me.' When she broke down, Brandon jumped up and cuddled her, trying to reassure her, telling her it was going to be alright.

"It's those two I worry about," she said, staring at her kids, "Kipper could be a right bastard sometimes… He was always scrapping. People just wound him up, but he was a good dad," she said, trying to reign herself in. "Now they haven't got a dad… Sorry," she apologised to me, drying her eyes.

Nodding, I looked down; I didn't know what to say. One stupid action and the dominoes fell. Everyone was paying for this. The Duggens, Kipper, Trace, his Kids and for what? Nothing!! That's what. The whole thing was bullshit, just a waste of time, a waste of people's lives. Kipper had come out after me and Danny with a fucking baseball bat and ended up killing a kid. I hated the cunt, but it wasn't that simple, not now. Looking at the kids playing behind me, I felt bad for them. They were the real victims of this. Talk about the sins of the fathers.

Brandon's voice brought me back from my thoughts: "So, you're Skinner, Tank's mate from the dig?"

"Yeah, that's it, the dig," I nodded.

Everyone in the room was watching me now. It was time for me to join in, have my say, let people know I was alright.

"So, where's Lenny the Lamp?" I asked.

The whole room broke into riotous laughter. I looked at Renny; he grinned.

"I'm Lenny the Lamp," he informed me.

"No, I'm Lenny the Lamp," shouted Robbo.

Trace giggled, declaring, "No, he's not, I'm Lenny," followed by Brandon and the other girl.

Once the room had settled down, they told me that Lenny was dead. He had died two years ago in a motorbike accident. He had been having a burn-up with another bike on the A414 and he'd lost control, come off the road at about 80 miles an hour, and got wrapped around a lamppost. Sue, his girlfriend, the other girl in the room, had been devastated by his death at the time. After his funeral (a proper bikers send-off), she found out that as Lenny was the sitting tenant of the flat, there was a possibility that she might lose her home of the last five years as the council had stopped giving flats to single people years ago. Because of this, she hadn't informed the council of her change of circumstances: 'Lenny's benefits had come in handy too, especially as he was on the disability too' she'd said, with a smile playing at her lips.

To start with it had been easy to cover up, just a few forms to fill in, a few forms not to fill in, then the day came when the Council wanted to pay a visit, check everything was OK in the flat. Sue was in turmoil, she wanted to come clean, throw herself on the mercy of the Council, maybe they'd let her keep the place after all, but Brandon wasn't having any of it. He'd been living there with Sue as a couple for a while now. He wasn't going anywhere. So, he became Lenny for the day, and any other day the silly twats put in a visit. Sometimes, 'the Brandon Lenny' wasn't around, so Robbo would be Lenny for the day.

I felt like a right berk. Everyone knew he was dead. Everyone on the Farm, in the local pubs, the local parish vicar, even the registrar of Births, Deaths and Marriages knew of his passing. Everyone apart from Herts County Council and me.

"I'm Lemony the lamb," screeched one of the little kids playing behind the sofa, and the room, including me this time, dissolved into laughter.

Renny stretched and stood up with purpose. "I'm off, you coming Skinner?"

Nodding, I got up, edging the teacup with its floating pea further away.

Brandon sniffed, "I'll let you know how much we get for the smellies, should be an Ayrton Senna at least Renny, see ya later."

Renny and me said our goodbyes and walked back into the hallway where he stopped me. He bumped open a split graffitied door. There sleeping soundly on one side of the room, in a circle of dogs was Hillsey. A hand brushed absently at his brow, then he farted and rolled over, so he was facing away from us.

On the other side of the room, there were sheets of newspaper laid out which served as a dog toilet. Now I knew where the smell of shit was coming from; there were three fresh turds sitting on the front of the News of the World.

Renny grabbed his nose theatrically, creasing up laughing. I soon joined him. Fucking hell, it stank.

In amongst the mound of hair a low snarling sound emitted and Renny backed away.

Grrrrrrrrrrrrrrrrrr...

"Stinky fucking Terrier… He's been funny with me since I went out with Basher's sister Carol, the vicious little sod," he declared. "Come on, let's get out of here before he wakes up Sleeping Beauty and the other dwarves."

Grrrrrrrrrrrr...

Renny and me sauntered out of the flat into the fresh air on the Ridgeway.

"I've got Cleaver Massacre, Blancmange Anarchy, and Piledriver, at the Triad in Bishop Stortford tonight. Do you want to come along?" Renny coughed, pulling out a readymade roll-up.

"Nah, cheers mate. I'm waiting for a call; I'm hoping to sort my own band out."

"OK Skinner, up to you, if you change your mind, I'm at 93 Tudor Way. Just knock my door. See ya later."

"Yeah, see you Renny."

I smiled at my new friend, and started back for Longwood Road, the posh side of the estate, thinking about Legion of the Dead.

Legion of the Dead had started off so well. Whiff, Dave and me had carried on practising every week after Andy's departure, making ready for Sulli our new vocalist to join.

Sulli was well up for it. We had talked on the phone on many occasions, and I'd even mailed him the lyrics to 'Exhibition,' 'Church War' and 'Child A is Born' as well as a few of the Horror Tape tracks I was hoping to make Legion tracks, but with him being so far away it was difficult.

Days led to weeks, weeks to months, and after a while, Sulli stopped picking up the phone. His mum would answer, and I'd leave a message and that was it: no reply. Sulli lived in a shed at the bottom of his garden, so I wasn't that worried about it. I just focused on what he had said to me when we'd dropped the microdots in the Greenman Pub: 'Yeah, I'm interested, very interested, let's do it.'

In the meantime, with the months passing by, Whiff, Dave, and to a lesser extent, me, decided to audition a few other people, just in case.

Gobber was up first. For the most part, he sounded like a cat that had got its tail slammed in a door. It was fucking 'orrible. Strangely enough, after we had packed up our gear, he had told us that he had written some lyrics and asked if we'd like to hear them as if he'd got the gig. I told him 'No mate,' and 'you're not singing for us', which really surprised him. He asked for another chance, so we agreed, him being a mate and that, but it was no good. Even though we had given him another week to prepare. He was even worse the second time around; he was the same cat, but this time, instead of its tail, it was like it's bollocks had got jammed in the door. It was bass warping, drumstick bending and plectrum curling all at once.

Next came Mucus, to be fair he was alright, but he had a Saturday job, which wouldn't have worked for any of us. Then came Basher, who again, was decent enough, but after a few days of trying to phone him, to tell him he was in, I gave up, much to Dave's relief as he had seen him eyeing up the tools in the back of his van. Not long afterwards he must have been nicked for his glue raid on 'Tit Head Tarling's DIY shop, I guessed.

Whiff still reckoned the Cowardly Custer might be the right man, but Cerys had seen him in The Get Punched Up House on the night Robbo had tried his luck, and he didn't even pretend to be a punk anymore. He was a proper casual now.

Chris Almond was our last hope of finding someone who lived locally, and he didn't want to be a singer, he was a guitarist.

I knew how he felt. Playing guitar was all I wanted to do, but when the opportunity came for us to borrow Doggy's Fostex four-track I put myself forward for vocal duties. I soon found out that I wasn't good enough to play guitar and sing at the same time. It was hilarious, I was all over the place, I was fucking terrible. So, in the end, we decided we would record the music down at the pavilion while playing live, then I would record the vocals later on back at mine. The demo tape went:

1. Legion of the Dead
2. Church War
3. Exhibition
4. Revenge
5. Syndicate
6. City of the Damned

I was so happy with our demo, that I sent it away to Pooch, Discharge's guitarist, phoning him a few weeks later to see what he thought. Pooch was impressed; he said the music was brilliant, particularly the guitar, but when I mentioned the vocals, he said 'he'd better go' as 'his missus was moaning at him to take the dog for a walk.' That's when I first started having doubts about my vocals.

Whiff and Dave had been nothing but encouraging about them, saying they were 'OK' and 'pretty good Skin', 'you'll get better'. I wasn't convinced though, so I gave them a proper listen. I forgot it was me singing, forgot about what they meant, and thought about how they'd come across to someone else.

I thought they were OK, then it dawned on me. They were OK... if I was American. For some reason, I had sung them in a faux American accent. The more I listened, the more ridiculous it was. My vowels were straight out of New York. I had been delusional, overconfident, and because of that, time was running out. I had to sort out our vocalist problem and I had to do it quickly because in a quiet moment, Whiff had told me that if nothing happened with the band in the next month, then he was thinking of going to university – that was three months ago.

I couldn't believe it when he told me, I thought he hated the system as much as I did. Not only that, it was also like another ultimatum. Andy had gone because of him, and now that we didn't have a singer, he was going to piss off too.

Whiff was a mate though. I thought about it later, remembering how he felt about his first job after leaving school, working for Enfield Small Arms. He fucking hated it. It had put him off working for life, he reckoned, and a nice cushy three years at uni would be a lot more of a laugh.

I couldn't argue with him on that, the work was laborious in the extreme, and he was making weapons to sell to dictatorships all around the world so they could murder men, women, and children. It was a no-brainer really, I thought, good luck to you mate.

I put my key into the lock at 34 Longwood Road, turned it and wandered in, making Badwitch, who was standing in the kitchen, jump.

She formed a rictus smile.

"Hi, bye," she smarmed and disappeared upstairs.

Pete appeared from behind a cupboard door, and with a can of baked beans in hand, he rolled his eyes at his fleeing girlfriend.

"Hiya Skinner, before I forget, Doggy phoned. He said to phone him back... I'll leave you to it," he said, putting the beans on the cooker. "You won't be long, will you?"

"Nah, not at all Pete, cheers mate."

Pete set the gas on one and followed his girlfriend upstairs.

Doggy phoning was what I'd been waiting for. Sulli hadn't been taking my calls, but he'd been taking Doggy's. I thought if he was taking Doggy's calls then maybe he would meet up with him. It turned out I was right.

Doggy told me he was meeting up with the elusive Sulli tonight at his shed, that he'd definitely be there but he was out of petrol so, 'can you drive?' I thought, OK, that's the least I can do.

I bounded upstairs for a quick spliff before tea, passing the two students' bedroom, and heard Morrissey of the Smiths singing something about, 'how soon is now,' and I thought, hopefully, fucking soon.

Chapter Two

Cabbages

Onto my portable stereo went Venom's Black Metal album, and I lay back on my bed to wait the hour or so until I was due to go to pick up Doggy, gazing out of my west-facing window as the late summer sunset, turning the sky crimson.

Once I had stretched out and started to zone out, there was a sharp bang on the wall from the bathroom next to my bedroom, disturbing me from my reverie.

Badwitch was playing her silly little games again, trying to make it uncomfortable for the oik cuckoo in her house - hoping to get him out.

She'd been doing it since I'd moved in, smashing the light pull against my wall or slamming the door early in the morning. One time Pete must have heard the door slamming early too, as I heard him telling her to 'leave it out' and 'give him a chance' as they walked down the stairs. Not long after, the door slamming shut stopped, but the random bangs and crashes from the bathroom carried on still.

Snorting, I rolled over. I couldn't be arsed with her bullshit tonight, there were more important things to think about. I must have dozed off because when I opened my eyes, Kronos had stopped hailing Satan and it was almost dark outside.

Checking the clock, I saw I was late. Why was I always late? My old man always said that I'd be late for my own funeral. He was probably right, but I thought good, even better if I was late for my death. I grabbed my leather jacket, threw it on, stuffed my roll-up tin into the pocket. It was time to go - see what the fucking hell was happening with Sulli.

In the fluorescent light of the Farm, I sprinted up to my van, a muddy old Fiat Fiorino that the Manpower Services had kindly provided, jumped in, turned the engine over and got going, powering off.

On the way up the Ridgeway, I got a few strange looks, which wasn't anything new. It was a strange-looking vehicle to say the least, with its low sleek front and high square box on its back. It looked like a John Paul II's pope mobile with no windows in the back, I wasn't complaining though.

To tell the truth, the Manpower Service had saved me a lot of aggro. Once I knew for sure that my dad and mum were moving away, I had quickly passed my driving test and got a job as a roofer with a company called Argogrand. I was taken on as a labourer and driver with the promise of a company van.

On my first day, I was told that the van wasn't ready, so we'd have to use my Mini to go to the job, and that's how it carried on. I was really pissed off. One of the reasons I took the job in the first place was because my Mini was in a bad way. It had a hole in the floor of the shotgun seat footwell, and if that wasn't bad, all the underseals under the doors were rotted away. They had more holes in them than Emmental cheese; never in a million years would it have got through its next MOT, so I wanted to get rid of it as soon as.

In the week before dad and mums' move, low and behold a job came up through the Manpower Services, working on another architectural dig. I knew the score, so I was a shoe in. Even better still, a van was available and none of the usual dig suspects wanted it. I couldn't fucking believe it, why didn't anyone want the van? Then someone told me that the dig driver duties included driving the pissed-up workers back from the pub after getting paid on Friday. It didn't bother me in the least, I could still have a couple and drive. No big deal there.

Once I was signed up for another dig, I took great pleasure in telling my overseer Jeff and his stupidly named slave driver boss Roy Oneless, or Oneless bollock, as I thought of him, to stick their job up their arses. Unsurprisingly, they weren't too happy about that, as they had been expecting me to carry on driving them into London for their 'big job' at Chelsea barracks at the top of Kings Road. I found out later that they'd both been nicked for drunk driving, that's why they'd employed me in the first place. So, with no driver, they'd lost the contract for their 'big job.' Fuck them, I thought. If they'd treated me right and got me the van they promised, then I'd have treated them right. I wouldn't have let them down.

Now I had transport, it was time to get rid of the Mini before the MOT ran out. There was only five weeks left - time was of the essence. Taddy, Cerys's older brother, knew his way around cars. So, on a visit back to the village to see Cerys, Taddy and me filled up the holes in the seals with newspaper, sprayed over the top of them with black paint and rubbed a bit of mud on for effect. Then, we hid a bit of plywood under the near side carpet to cover up 'the Fred Flintstone Hole' and listed it for sale in The Hertford Mercury for £600.

A few days later I got a call from a bloke called Jacob about it. The bloke was really interested as he 'needed some wheels quickly.' I had to be careful though, at some point in the future, he'd find out about my little customisations. Not wanting to shit on my doorstep, so to speak, I arranged the viewing in the car park at Hertford North Station for that afternoon. Jacob and his mate Arnie met me in the car park as arranged and proceeded to wander around the car kicking the tyres, showing they knew nothing about cars. Having said that, if one of them would have known nothing about kicking and had hit one of the seals, they could've proven otherwise. Thankfully their kicks were true.

Jacob asked for a test drive. I told him 'No problem,' opening the nearside door and claiming shotgun, ensuring that they both got in on the driver's side. Arnie wasn't Arnie Schwarzenegger, but he was a fat bastard, nonetheless. The last thing I wanted was for him to put his size elevens through the floor and find out the car was built for Bedrock drivers.

Once the test drive was complete, we all jumped out and after a couple more looks at the tyres again, Jacob sucked air in between his teeth, shook his head, and informed me, "The MOTs nearly run out, I don't know if I want it." He smirked at his mate Arnie, who slyly winked back.

I told him it is what it is, and he pursed his lips, thought for a moment, and then offered me £500 for it. It was my turn for a bit of play-acting now. With a sharp intake of breath and a sniff, I dragged my hand down my chin.

"Hmmmm, don't know..." I told them, thinking, if Arthur Daley was watching this, he would have doffed his Trilby at this staunch, if slightly amateurish, performance. "Yeah, OK then," I murmured, like a man who knows when he's beaten.

Jacob and me shook on it, and after taking out five 20-pound notes from his bundle, he passed me the 500 quid, which is what I wanted for it in the first place.

Still looking a bit miffed by the transaction, still in full-on Arthur Dale mode, I handed him the keys, the service history, ripped off the V5C, giving him the part that said who the previous owner was (a one Mr Frank Baker of 3 Ducketts Wood Thundridge), thanked him, and got the fuck out of there.

I continued along the Ridgeway, ignoring the looks, drove on down Tudor Way, turned left on Welwyn Road, then right at the bottom of the hill, and out onto the A119, where I saw Renny walking away from the station looking pissed off.

Pulling over, winding my window down, I asked him what was up.

"The fucking trains are on strike," he raged. "You don't fancy going over the Triad do ya? There's six bands on now: Cleaver Massacre, Blancmange Anarchy, Piledriver, and they've added Calcified Christians, Chain Stoking, and The Banana Bastards," he told me, his face brightening.

"Nah, I'm going to Cambridge mate, see if Sulli still wants to sing for us."

"What, the Sickos singer? Can't believe they split up, saw them four times... Sound, they were. I'll come along - I could get a train from Cambridge to Storford?" he enquired, already reaching for the door.

"Yeah, why not," I told the little punk almanac, smiling broadly.

Renny jumped in, lifted his hands up and stared in disbelief. They were covered in mud. "Shit, look at the state of this, don't you wash this fucking van?" he moaned, scraping his hands under the seat.

"Nah, mate," I laughed, putting the van in gear and pulling away. "Me and Tank, the last Manpower Service driver, have got a bet on. He had the van for 6 months before he washed it; I'm not even halfway there yet," I explained while pushing Black Flags' 'My War' into the cassette player.

Renny cracked a smile, and we sat back listening to Henry Rollins exorcising the demons from his mind as I navigated the hazardous route through the back roads of Bengeo; the shortcut to the village. Not only was it hilly, but most of the narrow streets were double parked on both sides with all the car owners wanting to park directly outside of their houses. It was a nightmare for a new driver like me.

One particular street had a steep gradient with a T- junction at the top of it. If there was a car approaching from the top, you'd have to stop, wrench the handbrake up and sit there, squashed back into your seat, gaping up into the sky, like you were on the launch pad of Apollo 13. Then once the car had gone by, you'd have to pull off the hill-start from hell.

Thankfully, today it was all quiet at the T- junction and apart from the odd near miss along the walls of parked cars, we drove through without any incident.

Once we were through the lean streets of Bengeo it was plain sailing, out into the green fields of Hertfordshire. Chapmore End passed us by with Dr Barnardo's 'bad boys' school on the right. Then we passed Debbie Lee's, one of Dave's old girlfriend's house, with its horses and array of jumps. Finally, onto Anchor Lane and into Thundridge village. As we passed the village hall, I saw lights blazing, kids running about outside. I thought, of course, it's Thursday night: it's youth club.

Doggy met us outside the Sow and Pigs, as planned. Since I had moved out of the village it was always this way now. It made his life easier as he reckoned his mum, Elizabeth, or Lady Elizabeth as my old man called her, used to give him grief if I went around for him.

I introduced Renny and Doggy, and Doggy piled into the roomy back and stretched out, telling us about his day at the recording studio in Holloway. Renny nodded knowingly as Doggy mentioned some metal bands he had been recording.

I thought, fucking hell if these two start going on about bands, the end of the world will come long before they've finished. Smiling to myself, I got back to the driving.

On the hill down from the pub, I saw the kids still running about, playing outside of the youth club. Suddenly, Ronnie bolted out of the double doors with Dave in close pursuit. I tooted the horn and when he realised it was me, he froze, like I'd caught him dancing to an ABBA song. Dave gave Ronnie the wankers sign, while I braked hard and coasted up next to him.

"You OK Dave, what you up to?"

"Oh nothing," he said, looking into the van, then spotting Doggy peeping at him through the bars of the back, he snorted, "You're not going around with him now, are you?"

I thought, yeah, at least he's getting out of the village, trying to see a bit of the world.

I said, "Yeah, he's alright," fiddling with the gear stick.

Renny saw there was something up and leant towards Dave. "What's going on in there? Is that some kind of a youth club?"

Dave's face clouded over like a U.K. bank holiday, scrutinising this piss-taker in the dark cab.

"Yeah, we used to have some laughs in there didn't we Dave?" I told him, diffusing the situation.

Dave nodded. "So where are you off to then, Skin?"

"To see Sulli, you know our supposedly new vocalist?"

Dave smirked. "Oh really?"

He was fully aware of what was going on; he had felt the same frustration as Whiff and me at the start, but just like Whiff, he had been thinking of a plan B. Only his plan B wasn't about getting out of the workforce, it was immersing himself in it.

"One way or another I'll find out tonight mate, that's for sure," I said, sticking the van in gear, keen to get away.

"Oh well, I'll keep the old fingers crossed; you never know."

I put my hand up in a wave and floored it off down the hill.

"Renny mate, don't do that again."

"He was being a twat; I don't like twats," Renny spat.

"Dave's sound mate, believe me."

Renny frowned, turned away to look out of the window. I thought, he might be small, but I'd better watch him, he could get me into a lot of trouble.

Renny and Doggy nattered away about bands and recording techniques, while Greg Ginn weaved his creepy offbeat guitar riffs around Rollin's lyrics. I sat back in the unforgiving driver's seat, manhandling the ungainly Fiorino around the corners of the A10, thinking about my last visit to Cambridge.

Max Headroom had been full of the usual colourful characters. Steve Mackintosh, the actor, had been there and of course, Hermit John, who seemed to be a new man after his night out with me, Doggy and Sulli, after we had boldly gone where no sane person had gone on microdots.

Mia had been there too. To start with she'd been as cold as a snowman's bollock sack towards me and Doggy, but as big Bertha the bong did the business, she soon thawed out, especially when she saw Doggy wasn't besotted with her anymore.

In fact, the whole knob end/knob head debate had gone public. Everyone had an opinion on what the two names meant, even Mia. She thought it was hilarious.

On the border between Hertfordshire and Cambridgeshire, the glints and twinkles of light from the small hamlets and villages became less and the darkness nestled in around us. The sky seemed to be growing in size too.

Cambridge appeared in front of us, with its low-level lights of orange and white, but it was Sawston we were going to. I stopped telling people I was going to Sawston long ago because nobody knew where it was, so I'd always say, 'I'm going up Cambridge.' It was the simple option. I hoped Doggy was right about Sulli being in tonight. It would be a long way to drive for nothing.

I turned off the road into Sulli's driveway, hearing the familiar sound of crunching shingle under my tyres. Black Flag died as I flipped the ignition off.

Renny checked his watch and spat, "How long we going to be here Skinner? Remember I need to get that train."

"When I find out what's going on, that's how long," I spat back.

Renny scowled, threw the door open and retorted, "Let's move then."

I exhaled deeply, throwing my door open and thinking, this little prat is getting on my fucking nerves. I shouldn't have brought him along,

"You alright Doggy?" I asked.

Doggy was already out and walking, crunching on the stones. "Come on, who fancies a nice little smoke?"

Renny and me fell into line behind him, silently passing the rows of cabbages and Brussels sprouts at the side of the house. Doggy strolled up to the shed, inhaled a rich scent of hashish and tapped the padlock gently against the door, saying, "Hello, hello, is there anybody there? Let us in, oh great spirit!" like an incantation.

Sulli's pale face appeared around the shed door, smiled at Doggy, looked quizzically at Renny, then dropped like a stone when he saw me.

"Skinner!!" he exclaimed. "I wasn't expecting you."

"What's happening with the band Sulli?"

Sulli jolted forward as the shed door flew open behind him and another two punks joined him, glowering at us, dossing us out. One was short and bulldog like-with a Mohican, and the other tall and lanky with a Sid Vicious spike the same as Sulli's.

Sulli told the bulldog, "Don't start Savy, I'll handle this."

Renny moved up beside me and squared up to the lanky prat, who smirked down at him from his high tower.

"I'm sorry Skinner, I've joined another band, mate," he informed me, shifting uncomfortably.

Savy butted his head forward, "Yeah, Savage fucking Circle; the only band worth a fuck around here."

Lanky cracked up. "Yeaaaaaah," he cheered, still holding Rennys' eye.

Renny sniffed, grinning at the twerp.

Sulli put his hand up. "Savy, back off," he admonished him.

Savy wasn't backing off though, he'd been waiting for this for a long time, "And no fucker is going to poach our vocalist."

"Who the fuck are you?" I demanded, my patience running out fast.

"You don't need to know that. That's on a need-to-know-only basis. All you need to know is that Sulli is lead vocalist with Savage Circle, our band," he told me, nodding to the lanky bloke, who punched the air.

I searched Sulli's face, wondering: what the fucking hell's going on? Why has it come to this? One phone call would have sorted this problem out. One. Little. Fucking. Phone. Call. Now this wanker is giving it the big one.

Sulli wouldn't even catch my eye though, like it was out of his hands now.

Savy's eyes blazed. "I think it's time you lot pissed off now … You and the Legionnaires of Doris's, or whatever the fuck you're calling yourselves now."

"Wanker," I shouted, lunging at him.

Sulli jumped in between us, grabbing at us both, trying to separate us. I felt Savy's hand digging into the side of my neck, felt his breath on my face. I forced my hand around Sulli, got it under Savy's chin and pushed his head upwards, putting pressure on his windpipe. I felt his resistance dwindling.

"You cunt," he screamed, retreating backwards and away.

Sulli shouted, "Just leave it out you two, there's no need for this!"

"There fucking is! You go near Mia again and you're fucking dead," he yelled, putting his fists up. "Fucking dead!" he told me again, just to make sure.

Sulli sighed and turned to the lanky punk, whose eyes were still glued on Renny. "Ray for fucks sake, can you get him back in the shed. Go rack up a line, have a spliff. Fucking chill out. I'll sort this out."

Ray snorted, "Noooo, I'm more interested in what this cabbage-headed cunt is looking a…."

Before he could finish, Renny smacked him left, right, uppercut, and he toppled backwards like a sawn sapling.

Nobody said a word.

Apart from Ray's soft groaning, it was completely silent.

"Anybody else want some?" asked Renny, scanning the faces in front of him.

Still nobody said a word, we just gaped at him.

Renny snorted "Huh!! Posh wankers." He turned to me, "Can I go to my gig now, Skinner?"

Nodding my head quickly, I said, "Yeah, yeah, OK, Renny,"

"Sulli you're a wanker, you should have called me," I spat over my shoulder, and the two of us paced away, leaving the wankers to lick their wounds.

"Where's Doggy gone?" I asked.

Renny grinned. "He legged it when you and that Savy dickhead started."

"Oh well, no surprise there - he plays keyboard."

Renny broke a smile, then tripped forwards, almost going over. "What the fuck?"

I kicked into something round and solid, so I stopped.

Peering down into the gloom, I saw we'd inadvertently wandered into Sulli's old man's cabbage patch. I booted one of the dark green head-sized orbs, and it rolled off into the Brussels, taking out a couple of storks.

"Oi, Renny, that spaz was right, you have got a head like a cabbage," I laughed, picking one up, spinning it in my hand.

Renny eyed me, "What?"

"Chill out man... fucking hell... Here, check this out, I'm on Patch of the Day," I grinned, drop-kicking it into the side of the house,

"It's Stewart Pearce," I continued, commentating like Motty. "Oh, unbelievable, he shoots, he scores. It's a goaaaal!" I booted another one.

Renny slowly shook his head, smiled, and leathered one himself.

Creasing up laughing, I kicked a few more myself, watching them roll off, leaves flapping. Then Renny picked one up and cricket bowled it at the distant shed. It arced high rolling in the soft moonlight and bounced off the roof.

Renny fell about laughing, then we were both at it; it was irresistible.

Cabbages rained down on Sulli's shed like a new plague of Egypt. Renny and me must have launched a dozen at it, most of them hitting the target, bouncing off the roof, or glancing off the side.

No one came out though, so we left it and went back to the van, to find a shaking Doggy, about halfway through a spliff.

Renny and me piled in, still cracking up about the assault of the cabbages, and I turned the motor over, floored it and we got going.

Doggy and Renny silently toked on the spliff and chilled out, while I decided to pass on the green, trying to get my mind around what had just happened, and more importantly, where it left Whiff, Dave and me now.

If only Sulli had let me know earlier, we might have had a chance; maybe we wouldn't have been so exacting with our new singer, given one of the auditionees more time to get it right. He didn't though, and we didn't, because we thought we had the perfect frontman waiting for us. I should have known earlier, should have taken the hint when he stopped returning my calls, but by then, he was the only one in the frame.

Whiff wasn't going to wait around any longer, doing long shifts for short money, making guns to maim little African and Asian kids with. I thought higher education was for wankers and posh kids but the way he saw it, it was a way out, a way out from the mouse race and all the associated bullshit that went with it.

Dave was the opposite to Whiff and me, he relished the order of work and wanted to do it all the time. It kept him steady; he liked steady, liked the known, the safety of repetition, that's why he put down roots in the village at the age of eighteen. I was happy for the bloke, really. I was happy, he was happy with his lot. He wasn't going to wait around either. It was like the less I saw of him, the more he played house with his girlfriend Abbie, and the more he threw himself into his work.

In simple terms, it was over: we were done. Legion of the Dead was fucking dead.

I came back from my thoughts, feeling the bile rising in my stomach.

"Legionnaires of the Doris's" I mumbled to myself, then said out loud, "Who is that asshole, Savy anyway?"

Renny took a tug on the spliff, gave it a reproachful look and tossed what was left of it out of the window, where the wind swept it away, "He's the guitarist in Savage Circle. Seen them a couple of times, they're really good."

Great, I thought, cheers for that mate.

Doggy piped up from the back, "I'm surprised you haven't met him, Skinner, he's a regular at Maximum Headroom. He was the one Mia said she was going out with when she refused my advances in the Greenman on launch night."

I cracked a smile, rolled my eyes and thought, the poor sap still couldn't see she wasn't interested in him. I let him keep going though, why burst the guy's bubble? I'd just found out how bad that can be.

Doggy liked 'gassing' as he called it, after a spliff, so I sat back, half listening, nodding my head at the appropriate moments.

Doggy wittered on for ages, going on about Mia and 'launch night', then he got to something of interest, and I was all ears.

"Yes, where was I? Oh yes, Savy, of course. Sorry, fellows, I went off on one there didn't I? You might not know him as Savy ... his real name is James Saville."

Renny smirked, "What like the kiddie fiddler?"

"Oh, Yeah, I've heard of him; Hermit John mentioned him. He's the bloke who grows his own weed, isn't he? Good weed too. John calls him a Herbologist." I cackled, cutting across Renny, who gave me a look.

Doggy chortled, putting his head up to the bars, "Yes, a Herbologist. It's rather good, isn't it? John sold me this weed, here, so it's probably grown by him… His dad runs a company called Tropical Splendid. They supply tropical plants to all the big banks in London. Check this out, he grows his weed in a greenhouse with his old man's yuccas, leopard lilies, bromeliads, and cheese plants…. He's a cl-"

Suddenly, Doggy realised he had said too much. Way too much.

Renny creaked forward in his seat, span round on Doggy, "And do you happen to know where this company is?" he demanded.

Doggy fell back from the bars, "Oh no, no, no, no way," he implored, then aware of who was asking him, and the considerable damage that he could unleash, he swallowed hard, "Y-y-yes, Renny. It's on a plot of land, just outside of Buntingford, in a village called Great Hormead."

"I know where Great Hormead is, me and Dapper use the Beehive pub if we're up that way," I told them, sliding my foot on the brake, slowing us down. "Do you still want to go to that gig Renny?"

"What fucking gig?" he came back.

I nodded, spun the van around smiling to myself. Nice one, I thought, a bit of payback and hopefully, an even bigger bit of weed.

Chapter Three

The Harvest

Great Hormead was a good place to grow weed, especially if your old man had a greenhouse full of tropical plants to grow it with.

It was a quiet little hamlet of about a hundred houses, with a garage and a pub, the Beehive. No police, no one interested in what anyone else was up to. The word sleepy didn't do it justice; comatose was a better word for it.

I'd been up there on several occasions with Dapper, whose mate, Jezz, lived in one of the cottages as you entered it. Jezz was always moaning, he couldn't get anything to smoke this far out in the sticks, so Dapper and me, being the benevolent kind, would go up the Frontline score a few bags of weed, and drop in on him to sell him a bag or two. In light of what I'd found out, it was weird to think that there might be a whole greenhouse full of it so close to him, maybe, even only a stone's throw away. It could have all been bullshit, but it was worth a look.

Renny, Doggy and me took about an hour to get there from Sawston, then another half an hour to find the tropical plant company.

Mr Saville senior had been clever with the security for his firm - he had absolutely none whatsoever. No lights, no barbed wire fences, nothing at all.

Only a tiny dirt track, buried deep under a group of leylandii, leading off the main road, gave away its existence. I must have passed it four times. If it wasn't for Doggy's incessant griping, saying we should go home, I would have missed it a fifth time, but his constant whining made me pull into the track to tell him to shut up. Navigating the high square back van through the stratospheric conifers, I saw something glint in the distance, maybe half a mile away. I hit full beam, saw the shine of glass from the greenhouses, then quickly killed the lights.

Renny tilted his head forward, "See that?"

"Oh yes," I sniggered, clicking off my seat belt.

Renny put his hand on my arm, "Turn around, so we can get away quicker,"

"OK, yeah, good idea," I replied, swinging the steering wheel around.

Doggy whinged, "This isn't a good idea, fellows. I've plenty, come on let's go."

"Nah it'll be fine, come on," I insisted, parking the van facing towards the road. "OK?" I asked Renny.

Renny sniffed, opened his door, stopped, then flipped the internal light off.

"Hold up, you got any tools?"

"There's a screwdriver in the glove box," I informed him, distractedly.

"Please, I don't…" begged Doggy.

"Come on Doggy, it'll be laugh, mate."

Doggy tentatively opened the van's back doors, slowly dropped his feet on the dirt track like he was the first human being stepping on Mars.

Once the Doggy had landed, he tip-toed over to a five-bar gate, cautiously leant on it and I sidled up next to him.

"Boo!" I mocked, grinning at him.

He gave a nervous laugh, "Sorry, this isn't my thing."

"Don't worry about it. Renny knows what he's doing," I said confidently, taking in the view under the haunting radiance of the moon.

In front of us, the track twisted down through a deep cornfield to three enormous, elongated greenhouses. On one side of them, to the left, there were a couple of wooden buildings that looked like chicken coops, then on the right, there stood a sizeable farmhouse with the shadow of a barn peeping out from behind it.

A couple of roebucks barked in the distance, calling and responding. A gentle breeze teased the rows of corn. It was beautiful. I started thinking maybe Doggy was right; we could have a puff in the van, then stand here and let it wash over us.

Renny had other ideas though, he couldn't have been happier. His mind was on the job at hand. He marched up to us, telling us that the best way to get to the greenhouses was to go through the cornfield away from the house, which sounded good to me.

I thought, what was I thinking? This is going to be fucking brilliant! So, I hopped over the gate and followed the mad little bastard.

Renny and me swished through the corn, leaving tracks in our wake, while Doggy trudged behind us, mumbling to himself. I wasn't a tough guy, by any measure, but I didn't understand how anyone of our age could have so little bottle. He was quite literally shaking in his shoes.

I shook my head and turned back to Renny, "So, you've done this before then?"

"What burglary? Yeah, a few times."

"Me too," I boasted, falling into line with my fellow criminal.

"Got nicked when I was 15, got three months, I was well pissed off."

I slowed down, checking his face. He wasn't messing about.

"Yeah, I bet," I said, solemnly.

"I wanted to get 6, the ones with more time pick on the ones who get a minimum, especially if they're my size," he said, lost in thought. "I could have got out after 2, but that would have meant going to another borstal, I didn't want to do that. I was established, didn't want to start all over again, that's the tough bit, letting people know you can't be messed with," he explained, pushing his hand back through his short spikey hair.

I nodded thoughtfully. Now I know why he smacked that lanky prat like it was nothing. It was normal for him, like it was just another part of life.

Doggy mumbled something unintelligible behind us. Renny and me cracked up.

"I don't know about you Skinner, not yet anyway, but they'd make mincemeat of your mate behind the door."

Doggy whimpered some more, just to prove his point. I'll give him his due though, he didn't turn back. He was still doing it, despite his tremors.

On the road behind us, a car came into view with full beams, bathing the countryside with light, rubber tyres hissing on the ash felt. We stopped, then ducked down, watching it as it approached the huge leylandiis. It disappeared behind them and reappeared almost at once, then it was gone.

Renny edged ahead as we came to the first of the greenhouses. Pulling at the sliding Perspex door, he found it wouldn't shift. I carefully moved up next to him, looking in through the Perspex into the inky darkness. Renny slid the screwdriver out from his German military jacket, wedged it under the shiny padlock hasp, put a bit of weight on it and it popped up in his hand. He slid the door open, his white teeth grinning at me, and we went in.

A few moments later Doggy joined us. I guessed that he must have realised he was less likely to be seen in here. It was more than that, though. Doggy started sniffing the air like he was a Bisto kid; he was completely enchanted by it.

"Oh, wooowww can you smell that," his face was luminescent.

I cackled to myself, thinking, typical Doggy. His love of cannabis overrides his fear of doing anything dangerous every time.

Renny saw it too and we exchanged a glance.

"Let's find the stuff and get the fuck out here," I whispered, and wandered off down a row of huge log-like plants, with tufts of green shoots on the top of them.

"No, Skinner, it's this way. They're over here somewhere," said the Bisto kid, his nose still in the air.

I cracked a grin and wiped my brow, fucking hell it was hot.

In front of me, I could just about make out a sliver of moonlight glimmering around a blind. Doggy was already walking. He paused, took a sniff, nodded his head like a nodding dog, then heaved the blind up. Then, the pong really hit me. I've never smelt anything like it before in my life. It actually made my eyes water.

Doggy started doing a little jig, which Renny and me soon joined in.

A few moments of merriment ended abruptly when we started talking about how we were going to get these plants safely back to the van. I counted twenty plants - maybe there were more, all in separate pots, all six-footers.

In the end, we went for a mixture of brute force, ignorance, and speed. Doggy, Renny and me grabbed two plants each, tugging them up out of their pots by the roots and banging the soil off on the floor. We had to get moving.

Back outside in the moonlight, I gave my two charges another good shake, making them lighter still, and moved back towards the field.

Suddenly, all hell broke loose in one of the hen houses - wings flapping, clucking, screeching. Geese streamed out of the other one, waddling towards us, honking. One of them approached Doggy, who went all Doctor Doolittle, trying to talk to the animals, shushing it. It wasn't interested in making friends with this intruder. Waddling passed him, beak open, it turned and struck, goosing him on the arse, jolting him forwards. Renny cuffed its head, and the little fucker honked off.

I cracked up laughing until a torch light zig-zagged across the field. There was a shout, dogs barked, and we were off on our heels, whipping back through the corn.

I heard a low menacing bark. I thought, oh shit. Looking around, I saw a dark shape cutting through the corn towards me. I stopped, brandished one of the cannabis plants and raised it up. As the dog came at me, I smashed it down, stopping it in its tracks. Growling, the dog eyed me for a moment, getting ready to come again, then Renny came tearing past me, and booted it hard in the ribs. It yelped, licked its side, dropped its head, and disappeared back into the rows.

"Come on Skinner! We need to move, look!" he warned, pointing a white finger towards the farmhouse.

A small white flat-back van was turning around in the farmyard.

Doggy got back to our van first, then Renny, then me.

I chucked my plants at Doggy, ran around the side, found I couldn't get the key in the door; my hands were shaking so much. Finally, finding a bit of composure, finding the keyhole, I twisted, the doors unlocked, and we all jumped in.

Renny shouted, "Go, go, go, fucking go."

I floored it, and we bounced out onto the road, heading for Royston.

"Fucking hell open the window will you Renny that fucking shit stinks," I called out over the screaming engine.

Renny frowned, catching his breath, and wound the window down.

The flat-back truck appeared on a side road. Zipping past it, Renny and me shared a glance of horror.

A few seconds later, we were lit up by full beams. I changed down and, stamped on the accelerator, but the ungainly, underpowered Fiat hardly gave me anything, and our pursuers started making ground on us. By the time we came into Barkway, they were right behind us. I couldn't believe how close they were, I could actually see into their cab. There were three of them. I could almost make out their faces.

"How are they so fucking close?" I bawled; eyes glued to the scrolling road.

"They're not, it's one of those Hyundai Cabstars, it hasn't got a bonnet," Renny shouted back.

"Yes, they fucking are," I yelled, glancing in the rear view mirror.

One of them was waving something about.

"What's that cunt got in his hands?" I said, missing the apex of a corner, then throwing the van hard left to correct it.

Doggy wailed in the back, "AAAaaaHHHHHaaaaa."

"Keep your eyes on the fucking road, Skinner," ordered Renny.

"He's got a shotgun," whimpered Doggy, from the back, "He's got a shotgun!!!"

I looked again. The van swerved towards the bank.

"THE ROAD. THE ROAD. WATCH THE FUCKING ROAD!" Renny shouted.

"I AM WATCHING THE FUCKING ROAD. SHUT UP!" I raged back.

"They're going to hit us!" cried Doggy.

Renny turned to me. "You'd better do something, Skinner. I can't save you this time," he said coldly.

Up ahead, there was a lorry slowly making its way up the brow of a hill. I changed down and stamped down hard on the accelerator, giving it everything. We raced up towards it.

Renny tensed in his seat, "Skinner!!"

"Skinner!!!?"

"SKINNERRRRRRRRRRR!!!!"

I snorted at the little tough guy, spun the wheel hard right and we missed the lorry by inches.

My eyes immediately went to the mirror.

The Cabstar fish tallied, braked hard. Then both pairs of headlights disappeared as we cleared the brow of the hill.

A few moments passed. I checked the mirrors: nothing. Checked again, and again, my eyes bouncing from the mirrors to the rapidly scrolling road. There was nothing behind us and an empty road in front.

Inside the van, I heard nothing but the rolling tyres. Even Renny was silent, pitched back in his seat, just staring ahead. Then a low groan emitted from the back. Doggy's head slowly raised up from behind the bars.

"What happened?" he asked, his voice trembling.

"Skinner lost them didn't you Skinner?" replied Renny, rapidly composing himself.

Exhaling, I nodded my head, easing off on the accelerator.

Renny sat forward, "Did they crash?" he asked, nonchalantly.

"What? Nah, don't think so... They just gave up."

"Fucking hell, I thought we were going to hit that lorry," he laughed.

Doggy wriggled his head through into the cab and gibbered, "They had a shotgun Skinner, did you see that? They had a bloody shotgun…"

"Yeah, I saw it, Doggy… I saw." I told him.

"Who were they, Skinner?"

"Fucked if I know."

Renny rocked forward, "Come on, let's not wait around and find out."

I checked the mirrors one last time and put my foot down.

Chapter Four

Friends, Romans, Countrymen

In the small hours of the next morning, I woke up hot and sweaty in my bed, thinking of the chase, the Cabstar, the bastards in the cab waving their shotgun at us threatening us and what could have happened.

It felt like they had been in pursuit all night long; the panic, the helplessness, the feeling of mortality, and of course, the rage I had felt sitting in the driver's seat had invaded my dreams. Strangling them, poisoning them, turning them sour, making my head ache, my stomach tight, swollen with bile.

I was exhausted with it all, but dwelling on it wasn't an option. It was time to put it to bed. I couldn't do anything about it now; what had happened, had happened. So what!! We'd got away clean and clear.

Once we'd made it back to the Farm, Renny and me ditched the plants at his nan's allotment, hid them in her greenhouse amongst her tomato plants. Now we had our own greenhouse of weed; they were ours as long as we kept our mouths shut.

Nah, fuck it. I couldn't be exhausted. Not today. I had a full day's work in front of me. It was the start day of the next dig.

I couldn't wait; this would be my fourth dig. The previous three had been at 'Foxholes', near the Pinehurst estate in Hertford. Baldock Street in Ware was the next place to be investigated.

Builders had dug up a load of Roman artefacts behind the Indian restaurant. Surprisingly, they hadn't tried to knock them out themselves. Instead, they had contacted the Hertfordshire Mercury, who in turn contacted Herts Archaeological Unit, and after securing funds from the Manpower Services, the dig was on. I loved the first day of a new dig, you never quite knew who was going to show up.

Every reprobate I could think of had done at least one dig. Tank, Viv, Paranoid John, Hippy John, Psychobilly, Dirty Den, Aiden, Karen Smith, Gary Flood, Will 'Womble' Wiseman, Maggie Heap, Chris Almond, Pat Cottis Nicky Kuczek, Mark Harper, Muncher Holtby, Steve Bartlet. I was sure I would be seeing some of them again, as like me, they were qualified.

Qualified long-term unemployed.

I sat up in bed, feeling a lot better, thinking, if Hertfordshire Police Force came in numbers today, big fucking numbers, and buried all us diggers under the remains of the Roman Empire, then crime in Hertford would be cut in half.

There was a soft tapping on my door.

"Skinner? Skinner?" It was Pete. "Phone, mate."

"Cheers Pete," I responded, sleepily.

Who the fuck is calling at this time of the morning? I thought, chucking my duvet off, getting myself moving.

In the kitchen, Badwitch fired a scowl in my direction, said her usual, 'Hi, bye' and promptly walked out. I picked up the phone from off the worktop.

"Hello?"

Doggy let loose in my ear. "Sulli phoned asking questions about last night," he whined.

"OK mate… Don't worry, keep cool," I said, trying to calm the bloke, "What did he say?"

"He asked if we'd come up in my mum's car."

Now it was my time to panic. What had the stupid hippy said?

Twisting the extra-long phone cord in my hand, I asked tentatively, "And what did you say?"

Doggy inhaled deeply, "I said, yes."

"Oh, nice one, you little beauty, if you were here, I'd kiss you. That's amazing mate."

Doggy laughed, "No thanks… I don't know if he believed me or not though, Skinner."

"Did he say he didn't believe you?"

"No, no he didn't… but…"

"What else did he say?"

"Nothing much, we just talked about Savage Circle… They're really going places."

I snorted, rolled my eyes up to the heavens, then told him, "Well, there you go then, no problemo… Doggy listen!! They don't know a thing. Sulli was hiding from Renny in his shed, shitting himself, when we were in Great Hormead. He's just clutching at straws."

"Who were those people?"

"Fuck knows… a bunch of webbed-footed farmers?"

"Skinner, it's not funny. They had a bloody shotgun," he said in hushed tones like he thought his mum was earwigging at his end.

"Yeah, so? We lost them, didn't we? End of story," I hissed back.

Badwitch came back into the kitchen, gave me another scowl, took a yogurt pot out of the fridge and strutted out like she'd caught me stealing from a nursery school. It looked like someone had been earwigging at my end too.

I thought, you stupid fucking mare, I'm getting pissed off with this. I've lived with unwarranted hatred for years now. I'm going to put a stop to it.

"Skinner? What's up?"

"Oh, Nothing. Nothing I can't handle."

I told Doggy I would be around with a present for his services in saving our hides, which cheered him up no end, and hung up.

I had to get moving, I was late again, so I grabbed an old baked potato from my part of the fridge. Chomping on its coarse skin, I legged it out to the van and got underway.

A few too many traffic jams later, I was taking a sharp right turn at the side of the Indian restaurant and pulling into their car park at the back. Immediately, like he'd been waiting for me, one of the staff came out and told me it was private property. I nodded, span the wheel, and parked it in front of some garages on the other side.

"Oi Skinner," I heard, as I jumped out.

In front of the long crew shed stood Tank. I flashed him the peace sign and wandered over to greet the big biker. Tank, or Alan Michael Slade, was in his mid-30s, had long matted hair and a beard, wore denim and leathers, and drank Abbott and Edie. Every weekend he'd be in the Black Horse, the biker's pub in Hertford, headbanging along to Motorhead, Saxon, and Iron Maiden.

Tank was a biker one hundred per cent, apart from one thing. He didn't have a motorbike. Poor Tank was in a catch-22 situation. Being the proud rocker that he was, there was no way he was going to suffer the indignity of getting a 100cc or 125cc, or worse still a 'fucking ped', or 'a suicide-inducing scooter.' So, he couldn't do his test. So, he couldn't get a bike.

Once we'd said hello and caught up, we strolled into the shed, noticing it was full of the next crew of diggers. Hugh, the dig's supervisor saw us and stood up.

"Right…Now we are all here, ahem," he said, giving Tank and me a look. "I would like to welcome you all to the Baldock Street dig. For those who don't know me, I'm Hugh Borill, and for those who do, keep shtum," he grinned, putting his hand up to quell the soft laughter from the diggers.

Hugh had a little fiddle with his moustache, then continued, "OK, so this is a very important dig, well, they all are… But yes … Erm, from what we have seen so far, the builders have dug up evidence of a Roman coach house, which should come as no surprise… Ware was actually on the route between London and Peterborough. Most of you will know that it was part of the magnificent Ermine Street, so there should be plenty of features…"

It was interesting that there had been people living here all those years ago, but right now I was more interested in who the next diggers were.

Scanning the room, I saw there was no Aiden or Dirty Den. No big surprise there. Den had been back to his old ways, and if Den was, then it followed that Aiden probably was too. There had been a rumour that Jason Brown would be starting today, but again, he wasn't here. No Mark Harper or Steve Bartlett either, more good news. I had been avoiding them both since Harlow and the aggro with Kipper and the Duggens. My eyes carried on around the room: Viv, her girlfriend Astrid, Nicky Kuczek, Paranoid John, Hippy John, Katherine the Catholic, Pat Cotis, Muncher. It looked like it was just the usual bunch, then I stopped.

William 'Psychobilly' Cox, another Farm resident, sat in a wheelbarrow watching Hugh, wearing a lopsided grin. I hadn't met him before, but Renny pointed him out to me one day, told me he was a fucking nutter. He lived down near the old people's flats, and he had this thing when they used to shuffle up to him. He would lie down, put his leg behind his head and say things like, 'Have you got four exhaust pipes for a Cortina Fastback?' or 'If you're going to the pet shop, don't buy the fish, they're all gay.' I watched him for a while - he seemed to be miles away - then came back to Hugh who was just winding up his introductive speech.

"So, that's it, let's get the top cleared off, about four feet should do it, and then we'll get our trowels out and see what we can find… Oh, and if we work hard enough, we should be in the pub by lunchtime," he said, beaming at us.

"Excuse me Mr Huge Bovrill?" enquired Psychobilly, "What shall I do after I've finished with fwa wa wa wa?"

Hugh didn't even raise an eyebrow. "After you finished with the fork, you can help Tank and Skinner, shovelling."

Hugh had obviously met him before.

Tank and me had a bit of time before we'd have to start the shovelling and barrow work as Hugh and the two girls, Viv and Astrid, had to measure the area which was to be dug out.

Tank took out his battered BSA roll-up tin, chucked me a readymade, and sparked his own up, inhaling deeply.

"Can you imagine them two going at it?" he smiled, scrutinising Viv and Astrid's peach-like backsides, as they bent over pushing the dig edge markers in.

"Yeah, that would be nice, wouldn't it, what a waste, eh?"

Tank creased up. "Look what I've got," he pronounced, pulling a copy of Men Only from his oil-covered denim cut-off. "I'm going to put it in Viv's bag."

"Tank, leave it out man, it's too much," I warned him shaking my head.

Tank took a quick, 'I'm so obviously up to something' look over at the girls, saw they still had their backs to us, and speed walked over to the shed. After taking another furtive look over at them he disappeared inside.

Moments later he returned with a mischievous grin on his face.

Once the markers were in place and the string threaded around them, showing us the outer edge of the dig, it was time for the hard work to begin. Everyone grabbed a shovel, formed a team of three and got stuck in.

Psychobilly, Tank and me being one team. Psychobilly was on forking duties, while Tank shovelled and I barrowed the loose soil, adding it to the slag heap that the builders left behind, at the back of the Indian restaurant.

It was the perfect day for it. The sun peeped through the clouds above us, its rays gently warming our backs. The soil was good too as it had been quite a wet summer, which meant it gave easily under the pressure of our forks and shovels.

Not only that, the builder's JCB had loosened it up as well before they had found evidence of the Roman coach house.

Progress was fast and the slag heap soon covered up the view into the kitchen at the back of the Indian restaurant. Some of the smells coming from there were amazing, intoxicating. I sniffed the air deeply, taking it down, inhaling it all, like I was tasting the food for the first time.

Cerys and me had our first Indian meal in there. The food had been great, but I had made a complete prat of myself by thinking the pickles served with poppadoms was a dish and struggled to get all the lime pickle down. It had blown my fucking head off, much to Cerys's amusement.

Clouds of smoke wafted up behind me, disturbing me from my thoughts, then I was choking, like I was back on the lime pickle again. I turned to see Nicky Kuczek had lit a fire under the nettles and the brush we had cleared off the site.

Next to him, Pat Cotis was feeding it with branches left from the tree the builders had cut down. In fact, he was throwing everything on, everything he could get his hand on. Pat only had one arm, had a fake one with a hook on the end, but that didn't stop him from getting stuck in. The fire was roaring, hazing the people standing around it.

One of them was Tank, he was grinning at me. In his hand, he was swinging a small bag backwards and forwards over the fire, "Oi Skinner, do you want your sandwiches toasted?"

"What? …Oi, you knob head," I laughed, running over.

Tank gave me a massive smile, went to dip the bag into the flames, and I snatched them out of his hands just in time.

"Fucking hell Tank, leave it out, I've got nothing else to eat."

"Like I would have done it… Come on, Skinner," he pleaded his innocence. "I'm not like that, it's only a windup," he smarmed, then went to grab the bag again.

I parried his grab, raising the bag up behind my back, so the asswipe couldn't get near it, and we both creased up laughing. Right, I thought, if you're going to try to wind everyone up, you're going to get some back.

Tank and me slouched back over to our trench, and got back to it. I thought it was time for a change, so I picked up the shovel, indicating to Tank that it was his turn on the barrow. You had to watch Tank; he'd always be looking for the doss.

Psychobilly looked around, "Shall I just carry on with this then, then, then?"

I threw a shovel full in the barrow, clods of earth hitting Tank. "Yeah, if you're alright with that mate," I replied, ignoring Tank's protests.

"If you say so, so, so," he told me.

"So," I told him.

One last shovel full and the barrow was full, Tank heaved the barrow up and fast walked over towards the small hill-like slag heap.

"Billy, grab some mud mate," I said, rolling a clod round in my hand, gesturing towards Tank as he disappeared behind the heap.

Billy grabbed a lump, rounded his too, and waited for the signal,

Pulling back my arm, I said, "Fire," coldly and lobbed my mud ball.

Suddenly, the air seemed to be full of mud. Creasing up, I turned and saw a lot of the other diggers had taken the opportunity to hurl mud at the windup merchant too.

In the hail of mud, a hail of abuse, then laughter, came back to us from behind the slag heap, and we all ducked down in our trenches.

A few moments later Tank's despondent face loomed large over the top of our trench. "Not funny Skinner, a stone hit me in the eye," he said, glumly, rubbing said eye.

Oh, no, I thought, jumping out of my trench, hoping he was alright, but he fell about laughing, and so did everyone else.

Tank grinned, "Oh Skinner, you're so easy."

Viv popped her head up from her trench, cooing, "Leave him alone, Tank."

This made him laugh even more.

Hugh popped his head up from his trench, "Enough of that now, clean up your loose soil, it's lunch."

Hugh's earlier idea about a pub lunch turned out to be a non-starter. Nobody had any money, so we sat back outside our shed, enjoying the early afternoon sunshine.

Tank and me sat down and made a little circle with Viv and Astrid.

I knew why he wanted to sit with them. It wouldn't be long until she discovered Tank's little glossy present.

Viv slowly drew her sandwich from her bag and asked, "You got a bike now Tank?"

Tank grinned uncertainly, searching their glowing faces.

Astrid sang, "Get your motor running, get out on the highway, looking for adventure, wherever comes my way. Born to be wiiillddd," and all of us apart from Tank creased up.

"I've got one, I've got one!" he protested too much.

Viv, Astrid and me shared a glance. I picked up my sandwich bag, noticing some of the plastic had melted into the bread.

"I'm impressed mate. Hold on, what? Really? Bullshit!!"

"No, I'm not winding you up, I've got a Matchless G45, it's a classic piece of British workmanship."

Viv snorted, still unconvinced, "When are we going to see this Matchless then?"

"Not for a while, I've got stuff to do on it... It's in my brother's old bedroom at the moment... I'll get there," he said, confidently.

Viv, Astrid and me fell about laughing.

Tank gave us a lopsided grin, "What?"

"Matchless? I bet it's fucking wheel-less," I quipped, sending us all off again.

"You'll see, I'll be off to the coast the next bank holiday," he assured us.

Pat Cotis leant in, "What, on a super saver return from Hertford North?" he interrupted, finishing us all off.

"No, no, no, no," he protested then descended into laughter himself.

Once I had stopped laughing, I tucked into my sandwich, melted plastic bit and all, watching the others as the banter went backwards and forwards. I'd seen it a hundred times before. It was good to see that even though everyone was different, liked different music, came from different backgrounds, we all seemed to gel so well. My eyes stopped on Katherine. She was a strange one.

Katherine the Catholic, or Kath'll lick anyone, as Tank called her, was a fully paid-up member of the Catholic League of Decency. She came to work as a volunteer a few weeks into my second dig. On meeting her for the first her time, I thought she had been sent by the local church to save our souls, half expecting to hear the kind of bullshit spouted by Hilary Charmen or see copies of the Tablet or the Catholic Herald placed strategically around the sinner's crew shed.

Not a bit of it, she was certainly interested in us, that much was true. She fawned all over us blokes like some religious nut job, tactile and caring, always ready to lend an ear to people in need, but according to Viv, she wasn't interested in getting into our souls. It was getting into our trousers she was interested in.

I'd thought Viv was on the windup and no wonder. Looking at her, you'd think, no way. She actually looked like she was in her mid-fifties - done with all that kind of nonsense. She had milk bottle glasses, a trite shampoo and set, wore cameos and brooches and of course a huge crucifix, complete with the dying Jesus. The rest of her attire was straight out of my mum's wardrobe.

Viv was adamant though, told me to watch it with her; she was just biding her time, waiting for the right moment. I laughed at her, wandering back to my trench and thinking, that's out of order, she's harmless enough.

A few months later, on the Foxholes dig, in the bleak mid-winter, I found myself huddled down in my trench, digging furiously just to try to keep my blood flowing. It was more First World War Passchendaele than Hertfordshire. I had been in a hurry that morning, late again and hadn't brought my thermal gloves with me. Consequently, I had been moaning about my predicament since I got there.

Hugh was a patient man, but that morning he'd had enough of the whining punk rocker, so he had told me to go and warm up in the crew shed, and while I was there, to get the tea on for the rest of the freezing diggers.

I had smirked at the shivering Tank, thinking, ha, ha, ha, I'm on the doss this time pal, then popped my head up above the parapet, waited for the icy wind to abate, and when it finally did, I legged it across no man's land to the crew shed.

Inside, I found Katherine had already put the tea on, so I gave her a pleasant, 'hello', sat down next to the Calor gas stove, then put my hands on it, feeling the warmth. I was still shaking with the cold, my teeth chattering away. It was going to take a long time to warm up.

Katherine's face had been a picture of concern. After she had taken the whistling kettle off the small hob and set it down, she sidled up next to me and put her arm around me. Pulling me in close, she told me, 'Don't worry, I'll warm you up.'

Immediately, I started to feel the snug heat from her body, so I stretched my aching arms, leaned back, inhaled deeply, and found that she smelt of lavender water and bath salts.

"That's it, Skinner, you relax… Just relax… Is there anything else I can do for you?' she purred, slipping her hands in between my legs.

I was so comfortable, I didn't realise what was happening. Then her hand slowly crept up my leg, shimmying towards the two ice cubes in my frozen bollock sack.

Confused, I turned to her and stared into her eyes. Her milk bottle glasses made her look like Whiff's mum, Judy.

"Oh no, fucking hell. No," I cried, leaping up, and making my way to the door.

I've never run so quickly before in my life. If there'd have been a starving polar bear waiting to rip me to bits, rip my frozen bits to bits, I would have still gone.

As it turned out there weren't any polar bears outside, just a lot of diggers cracking up laughing at another one of Katherine's potential victims making an escape.

"Skinner??" asked Viv, bringing me back from my thoughts. "Are you still with us?"

I stopped staring. "Yeah, sorry Viv, what's happening," I asked.

Viv looked from me to Katherine, "You've had your chance," she laughed.

"Oh shame, who's next on her to-do list?"

Viv cracked up, and we both took a peek.

Nicky Kuczek seemed to be her next target. In amongst the happy chatter of the diggers, she was giggling, throwing back her shampoo and set, and brushing her hand across his leg. I didn't think she'd have to try too hard, when it came to women, Nicky was a Lemmy kind of guy. Quantity over quality.

"People, come on let's get back to it," announced Hugh, standing up with purpose.

Viv reached forward picked up her thermos flask and tried to push it into her bag. Finding resistance, she opened it up to see what the problem was, and there was Tank's glossy Men Only magazine. Viv frowned, slid it out. She turned to Astrid who shrugged her shoulders, then to Tank, who fell about laughing.

Now everyone was watching, waiting to see her reaction.

I held my breath, thinking, you've gone too far this time Tank.

Viv flipped the mag over and turned it to the middle page spread.,

"Hmmm, I'd definitely shag her, she's gorgeous," she chuckled, and everyone cracked up laughing. There were even a few cheers.

Hugh stretched, fiddling with his moustache, "Come on, people, it's time to get back to it, oh, and if you don't want that magazine Viv, I'll take it off your hands, purely for research, of course," he joked, reaching forwards, palms open.

Viv shook her head, "No way! This is mine," she grinned, holding it firmly to her chest.

Hugh smiled broadly, then looked at Tank. "Right Tank, I need to keep an eye on you," he said, half-jokingly. "You're working with me this afternoon. We're going to map the site out... Skinner, you're with the two Johns."

Tank got up, smiling from ear to ear. He knew he wouldn't be able to piss about working with Hugh but mapping out was a complete doss; no shovel required.

I slouched over to the two Johns, Paranoid and Hippy, feeling a bit hard done by, picked up my shovel and started digging. I knew it was going to be a long afternoon working with Paranoid John, or PJ if you were feeling polite, as he was one of the worst acid casualties I'd ever met.

PJ and Tank were good mates, but PJ was a gentler soul than his mate Tank, so instead of donning denim and leathers and joining the bikers with his pal, he joined the hippy/glam rock scene in the late 60s or early 70s. PJ had a story about all 'the 60s faces.' In his lysergic acid diethyla-mind, he had dropped acid with them all. Been on every march. Done every gig. Fucked every groupie. Done the lot.

Tank told me that it was all true, Tank was always on the wind-up though, so I couldn't be sure. Most of it sounded like bullshit to me. Boring, 'I've done this, I've done that' bullshit too, but one story I really wanted to be true was the one about him going to the first Glastonbury festival in 1970.

Pat Cotis, another older member of the dig, not normally a wind-up merchant, had told me that one, so there was a possibility that it was true.

To enhance the experience of seeing Marc Bolan for the first time. PJ and a group of his mates had dropped a particularly strong batch of LSD in front of the main stage just as the glam rock god had come on. A few songs in the acid had come on strong, in vast waves, pulping their brains; they'd been left helpless, whimpering, slavering like dogs, not even knowing which way was up.

PJ had totally freaked out, he couldn't take it anymore, and then for reasons only known to himself, he began running around the festival shouting, 'I'm a fire engine, I'm a fire engine,' into people's faces.

I had asked Tank about it too. He said it was true, and that's why some people used to call him Dennis, after the Dennis Sabre fire engine.

PJ seemed unusually quiet today, morose even. Him and hippy John were just steadily shovelling the soil into the barrow.

Suddenly, a huge sod of earth exploded in our trench. I was just about to tell Tank to fuck off when I spotted his big frame in front of the shed talking to Hugh.

Still, I said 'Fuck off' to whoever chucked it, and Jason Brown's grinning face popped up from the trench next to ours.

"Whoops," he laughed and dropped back down again.

"Is he on the dig?" I asked PJ, who just ignored me.

Hippy John put another shovel load into the barrow, levelled it off, spitting, "Yeah, afraid so, him and Ridsey. He was supposed to start this morning - they just got here, bummer or what?"

PJ hoisted the last shovel load into the barrow, giving me the nod. It looked like I was on barrow duties as well. Sighing heavily at the injustice of it all, I hauled the barrow up, put my weight on it and pushed.

I checked out our neighbours as I walked along past the next trench. It was Jason Brown alright. I had seen him about on the Farm. He strutted about like he owned the place, and it was no wonder really - he was built like a brick shit house. He liked to show it off too. If there was a glimmer of sun, he'd be in shorts and have his shirt off; today was no different. He stared up, dossing me out as I heaved the barrow past until I finally came up onto the slag heap.

Upending the barrow, I quickly emptied the earth out then put the barrow over my head in readiness for the usual barrage of mud from the other diggers.

Soon it rained down. In amongst the soft clods of earth, half a house brick bounced off it, jarring me, making me drop to my knees.

Chucking the barrow down, I marched back around the slag heap.

"Who threw the fucking brick?" I demanded.

Viv stood up, in her trench, pointing at Jason Brown, "Who do you think it was? It was He-Man over there."

Jason Brown jumped out of his trench and stormed over to hers, shouting, "You cheeky fuckin bint, what would you know?"

"I saw you throw it Jason," she said, squinting up at him on the parapet.

"No, I mean, what would you know about men? You fucking dyke."

Viv moved forward, furiously gnashing her teeth. From where I was standing it looked like she was going to bite his nuts off.

"Fuck off Jason, that's out of order."

Tank had heard enough. He calmly handed the map board to Hugh, casually strolled around the side of the parapet, walked up behind Jason Brown, and dragged his shorts and pants down around his ankles. There was a massive gasp and then everyone descended into fits of laughter.

Jason Brown was stunned. He stood there waiting for his brain to come up with a solution. Finally, it told him to pull up his shorts and get the hell out of there while he still had a bit of pride left.

Viv was holding her stomach she was laughing so much, "Bloody hell, He-Man, is that it? It looks like a maggot on a piece of moss," she told his retreating form, "I think I'll stay a dyke."

Hugh took a deep breath, "People, calm down, let's get back to it," he said, watching Ridsey following Jason Brown out past the side of the Indian restaurant.

"Oh … he's off too, is he? That must be the quickest resignation, I've ever seen."

Astrid grinned, "Short and not sweet," then quipped, "Like his cock."

***

On Friday at lunchtime, it was time for us to collect our pay. No one was sure why the Manpower Services paid us at lunchtime. Nobody asked them either, because once we'd been paid, we downed our tools and that was it for the week.

Hugh distributed the little brown envelopes and we set off for the Bull, the nearest pub, to talk about the week's findings.

It had been a good first week too.

Once we had cleared the topsoil away, we found several decent Roman features, including post holes, hard evidence of the coach house, and a possible bath house. I could only have a couple of pints, being the Unit's driver, so I nursed a couple of snakebites while everyone else got stuck in.

Soon the conversations changed from work to more pressing matters, like, who could drink the most Abbot Ale and not long after that, even more pressing matters, like who could actually get up and walk.

Hugh was the first one who needed a lift home, so after helping him up, I led him to the Manpower Services van and drove him home. Walking him to his doorstep, I rang his doorbell and legged it before his wife answered the door.

One by one they fell, then finally, as the bell for last orders rang out, it was just me and Tank. I was confused though, as when I left to take Viv and Astrid home, it had been Tank, Kath'll lick and Nicky. I wondered where they'd gone.

Tank put me straight on that one. He told me that just after I left, Kath'll grabbed Nicky by the hand, and they had disappeared into the men's toilet together. I didn't want to think about that as I had a bit of business I wanted to attend to, so I told Tank if he wanted a lift home, it was now or never.

Tank sunk his ninth pint, burping extravagantly.

"OK, let's go," he slurred, hauling himself up into a standing position.

Tank lived in Raynham Street in Hertford, so normally after the Friday lunchtime pub sessions, I would drop him on my way back to the Farm. You could always rely on Tank to be the last digger standing, so it worked out perfectly.

Once I'd helped the big biker to the van, I unlocked the doors, and we piled in.

I started the van up.

"I know you want to go home mate, but I'm interested in getting a Suzi 125 to do my test on - there's a bloke in Wareside who's knocking one out. It's only got twenty thousand on the clock, can you have a look at it for me?"

Tank leant forwards, quite literally creasing up laughing, "Wee, wee, wee, wee," he said, twisting his wrist backwards and forwards like he was revving up a moped. "No, it'z all good Skinner... I'll have a little goozy gander."

I nodded and spun the wheel, pulling out of the side road next to the Indian.

"What's going on with Kath'll lick?" I asked him.

Tank chuckled drunkenly to himself, "I wouldn't touch that with yours, Skinner."

I snorted, "Isn't there something in the bible about loving your neighbour?"

"She'z loved all her neighbourz," he guffawed, "I bet she prayz every night, 'Oh god, oh god, oh god, I'm coming!'"

Tank fastened me with his best interrogating stare, "I bet you've been in there haven't you?"

"No, I fucking haven't mate, I legged it."

"Nooo, you've been Kath'll licked… Licked by Katherine."

"Yeah, that's it, me, your mum and her had a threesome."

Tank smiled, "Zoundz good to me," he slurred absently, his head flopping forward. He folded his arms, started dozing in his chair, sucking in huge breaths.

I stuck my bootleg copy of Venom's album 'At War with Satan' into the cassette player, turned the volume up and put my foot down. By the time the first side was about halfway through, we passed the Wareside sign and entered the village, where I started looking around. After a few minutes, I pulled up in front of a small, detached bungalow, killed the motor, jumped out and casually strolled around to the back door of the property. I thought this is perfect, so I went back to the van to wake the slumbering Tank.

"Tank? Tank?? Wake up mate, we're here."

Nothing.

"TANNNKKKK," I shouted, giving him a shove. He started and opened a bleary eye.

"What!! …. What? …." He said from somewhere else entirely.

"The bike. You remember?"

"Yeah… Yeah… oh yeah, the little moped, Johnny Moped, weeee, weeeee. Skinner moped… I'm coming," he grinned, stretching his arms out.

I strolled back across the road and up the path to the bungalow's front door and waited, hiding out of the view of the front room window, watching Tank getting his act together. Finally, he got out of the van and gingerly made his way over the road and onto the path. When he was halfway up the path, I rang the doorbell.

"Oi Tank, the bike's around the back here, man," I told him, pointing into the empty backyard. Then I legged it around the bungalow and back out onto the street again, just in time, to see a short, grey-haired man open the door to Tank.

I started the motor, put it in gear, hit the horn, and sped off, watching Tank's gawking face follow me down the road and out of sight.

Nah, you're too easy Tank, I thought, laughing to myself.

Chapter Five

Cheech and Chong

Saturday morning on the Farm was great, especially after a hard week working on the dig. If it was warm, I'd throw off my duvet, climb out of bed, open my windows wide, get back into bed again, and listen as the estate woke up.

Firstly, I would hear the birds in the gardens of the houses opposite. Then the footsteps of people in the flat above as they started their day. Then finally, and probably best of all, the sounds of the kids playing in the community playground next to the junction between Longwood Road and the Ridgeway. Life was all around me. It felt good. I felt part of something. A big family all living together.

Sometimes, Pete's dad and mum used to visit. I could hear them chatting away in the kitchen below me. I couldn't make out what they were saying. I didn't need to, I just liked to hear the way their voices dove-tailed, how the conversation flowed.

Now and again, if I was feeling tired or down, it would make me think of my own parents. I had made it tough on them as a kid, and even though I had been fully behind their move to Cornwall, jacking my job in with Argogrand, the roofers, a couple of weeks before their move had put a lot of unnecessary pressure on them.

No work for a week, while I waited for my third dig to begin, meant I was hanging around the house while they were trying to get ready for the move of their life. For me it was great; it gave me time to tape all my singles and albums before I sold them to Whiff and Chris Almond. It gave me time to whittle down my belongings to one small suitcase, and most importantly it gave me time to get my head right. I was happy with the respite, but dad didn't see it that way. He thought I was mad walking out on a job before I'd secured another one, especially with all that he had on his plate, and pretty soon, the arguments started.

Suddenly, little disagreements turned into fully blown arguments.

I wasn't too worried about them - it was silly stuff really, and unlike the rows we had in the past, instead of the usual silent routines for hours afterwards, sometimes days, we soon forgot about them and got on with what we needed to do.

At the time I thought he was just biding his time, keeping the peace, knowing full well that he wouldn't have to put up with me for much longer. On the day of the move though, I found out that it couldn't have been further from the truth.

On April 16th, 1984, the three of us, mum, dad and me watched the removal van hesitantly making its way up Duckets Wood, our home for the best part of sixteen years.

"I bet they don't drive that bloody carefully when we can't see them," dad stated.

"I'm sure they'll be fine Pudge, stop worrying..." my mum turned to me, her eyes welling up. "Right Mike," she choked. "No, no, that won't do at all," she uttered like she was reciting a mantra.

Mum took a deep breath and steadied herself.

"I remember my father saying 'goodbye' to me when I went into the Wrens. We were at Paddington station. My train came in and I started to cry. He embraced me and said, 'No, no, that won't do at all.'"

Looking her in the eyes, I brought her in close, giving her a squeeze, and said, "He was right, mum, we'll still be under the same sun."

"Yes," she said, squeezing me back. Then, her vice-like grip was gone and she turned away from me, quickly climbing into dad's new car.

I felt a hand on my shoulder. Turning around, there he was, stern-faced, his hand out: "Good luck, Mike."

"Cheers dad, you too," I said pumping his outstretched hand, then as we broke off, he drew me to him.

"You look after yourself," he told me, his voice cracking.

"I will dad, I will."

"You promise?"

I pulled back, surprised by the amount of emotion in his voice.

Searching his face, I saw a vulnerable old man: tired, aged and ashen. It was my turn to reign it in.

"I'll be fine dad, believe me," I assured him grabbing his hand again, shaking it.

A few moments passed and we were still shaking hands. I really didn't want to let go and nor did he. It was like we were making up for lost time, lost time we could never get back again. Then, both of saw the folly in it, cracked up laughing and let go. With one flap of his hand, dad got into his Daihatsu Charade, turned it over and drove off, with mum waving all the way up to the top of the road.

Suddenly I felt very alone. It was a feeling that came back to me every now and again, and when it did, it was usually on these Saturday mornings.

Badwitch's heavy footsteps on the landing, brought me back to reality. I rolled over in my bed, knowing what was coming. Sure enough, there was a loud crack as she smashed the light pull onto my wall. I smirked to myself. It was time for her early morning shit. OK, I thought, you might think you're better than me, but I've been in the toilet straight after you and your shit stinks just like everyone else's.

While she was in the bog, I made my way down to the kitchen, grabbed a half-eaten Vesta pot noodle, devoured it, and made it back to my bedroom before she'd left the toilet. Fucking hell, I thought, she must be launching the Bismarck in there.

A crack on the wall, a slammed toilet door, followed by heavy footsteps on the landing told me the launch was over. I needed to wash and get myself going so I darted into the bog, mouth breathing, flung the window open, just in time to see Renny slouching through the yards down below toward my front door.

"You alright Renny?" I called out to the little hooligan.

Renny stopped and gazed up, scanning the block's windows. Spotting my head, he shouted, "Did you get the message?"

"Nope," I replied, hungrily taking in the fresh air. "I gave it to that snooty housemate of yours." He spat, shielding his eyes from the glaring windows.

Oh right, now it all makes sense, I thought, that's your new game, is it? You stupid fucking cow.

I had been around for Renny twice since we'd robbed the plants and both times he'd been out. I was beginning to think he was trying to do the dirty on me, but it turned out, he'd come around on Monday during the day, while I was working on the dig, left a message that he'd be 'busy most of the week with gigs' and to 'go around for him Saturday morning, early as I could.'

"Sorry man, I didn't get your message," I called down.

Renny rolled his eyes, told me he needed to get a few bits in the shop on Tudor Way and to come around his in half an hour.

I nodded, taking my time, still cherishing the fresh air, watching him dodge back through the draped washing in the yards.

A few minutes later, after I had added to the stench, Badwitch was back on the landing. Seizing the moment, I gently opened the bog door.

"Janine, why didn't you tell me my mate had come around?" I asked.

She simpered, "Oh yes, sorryyyy, I forgot," remembering it all too clearly now.

Pete appeared behind her from their bedroom, "What's wrong? What's going on?"

"Skinner is getting angry with me because I didn't tell him his friend came around."

"I'm not getting angry Janine." I declared, getting angry.

Pete looked at me, then back at his girlfriend, then at me again. Then finally, back at his girlfriend, who gave him a look.

"Skinner, I'm sure it was just a mistake," he said, scratching nervously at his chin and giving me an imploring look; he didn't want any aggro.

I said, "Yeah a mistake, Pete, no problem," in the most reasonable tone I could muster, which wasn't much and wandered down the stairs.

As I opened the front door to leave, I heard Badwitch hiss, "He was so angry, Peter."

I slammed the door behind me and got out of there, thinking, not only is she a stuck-up bitch, she's a fucking sly one too. I better watch her, or I could be out.

Head down, I pounded along Longwood Road, trying to think of ways I could get her back, stop her bullshit without pissing off Pete. I had already tried being myself and I'd fallen well short of her high standards. I had tried being overly nice, like how you'd treat your mates' parents, but that hadn't worked either. Not only that, it had left a bad taste in my mouth, I couldn't do fake. I strolled past her car, a soft-top VW Golf, and thought how easy it would be to slice the PVC with the Stanley knife I had in my van. I had all kinds of tools in my van. I could smash the fucking yuppy barrow to pieces, and it would serve the stupid stuck-up cow right.

Internally raging, I marched up the Ridgeway and onto Thieves Lane where I was so immersed in thoughts of revenge that I walked straight past Jason Brown. Something made me turn though. He threw a quick glance over his shoulder back at me and carried on. Fucking hell, I thought, he looks even bigger today.

A few minutes later, I was knocking on Renny's door. It opened straight away to reveal an old woman squinting at me.

I smiled, "Hello Mrs Reynolds, is Dean in?"

She smiled back, "Oooh, I'm not Mrs Reynolds, she was my daughter, she's long gone. Bless her, I'm Rennys' nan."

She shouted upstairs to Renny, who soon appeared behind her, a can of Tennent's Super in hand.

"I'm down here, you daft thing, I was in the kitchen, getting you a cup of tea, remember?" He told her, grinning at me.

"Oh, tsk! I don't know whether I'm coming or going these days," she laughed.

"You're a liability nan… See you later. Come on Skinner, this way."

Renny turned and I followed him into the house. Homely little place it was too. Deep shag pile carpets adorned the floors, and the walls were painted a bright yellow, covered with pictures of dogs, cats, and smiling kids on beaches. I followed him out into a long back garden. It was lined with small trees. At the bottom of them, shrubs grew competing with the surrounding bedding plants for sunlight.

I soon caught up with him, told him about Jason Brown showing up at the dig, Viv, the maggot in the moss and that I'd just seen him walking up my road.

"He's fucking massive." I told him. "I wouldn't want trouble with him."

Renny took a sip of the purple tin, "Yeah, he's big, but that doesn't mean he can fight, you just have to get in first."

I chuckled, remembering Savage Circle's drummer. How he went down like he'd been shot.

"So how did your gigs go," I enquired, changing the subject.

"Yeah, good. I've got a punk metal crossover gig coming up. Morbid Fridge, Thatcher's Minge and the Formica Murders."

I fell about, "Bollocks, come on, you're making them up. Thatcher's Minge aren't a band."

"They are," he insisted, "They come from Hitchin, supported Chron Gen a few times… I know their singer, Skelly, he's going out with Sue Slice, the drummer out the Jam Rags."

I shook my head, then did a double take. Jason Brown disappeared behind the garages at the back of the Ridgeway.

"And Morbid Fridge have been around for years. Their singer Uba must be in his forties now… What's up with you?"

"I think I saw Jason Brown; we'd better be careful."

"Skinner, stop shitting yourself about him. He's nothing," he told me, ending the conversation.

Renny and me walked to the edge of the estate, entered the allotment through an old creaky metal gate, then strolled down to the end to his nan's greenhouse.

Renny unlocked the sliding door, threw it back. "You're going to like this, Skinner."

I sauntered in.

I couldn't believe my eyes, the last time I had seen these plants, most of the leaves were split, some of the stems crushed – they'd looked like they were on the way out.

Not now though, they were totally unrecognisable.

All six looked lush, dark green, pristine, standing upright in olive green pots, with fresh dark soil at their bases.

Renny stood back proudly. "I'm into gardening," he winked.

"Fucking hell, that's amazing," I enthused, moving in to get a better look. I put my nose on one of the bud-like parts, the pong nearly knocking me over. "Whoa. Fucking hell!" I gasped.

"My grandad was into gardening, taught me all he knew," Renny explained. "Look, I've done some cuttings," he gestured.

In the middle of the greenhouse on an old chest of drawers, there were four seed trays, filled with the little cuttings.

Renny was in full flow now, telling me where to take the cuttings from and how you crushed the stem before putting it in the water with rooting powder. About soil PH levels, watering, light, flowering circles. He seemed to know everything. Not only was I amazed, I was surprised. I thought where plants were concerned, all you had to do was dig a hole, drop a seed in and wait a couple of months.

On and on he went, the little horticulturalist Percy Thrower. Seed germination, cloning, hybrids, Sativa, Indica, forced flowering; it was all very interesting, but I'd had enough, so I put up my hand to stop his flood of herbaceous knowledge.

There was only one thing I wanted to know. "When can we smoke it?"

"Not yet, I'm drying a few buds here," he answered, raising his head to the green bat-like leaves hanging above us. "If you dry it too quickly, it'll mess up the taste - it'll taste like shit. Another day should do it."

"Fucking hell, there's tonnes of it. It'd take Cheech and Chong two lifetimes to smoke this lot. What are we going to do with it all?"

Renny scratched his chin, giving me a sly look, "We're going to sell it."

Renny had that all worked out too. He would dry out the buds, roll them out flat with a rolling pin, cut them into pieces using his kitchen knife, weigh them using one penny as an eighth and two pence for a quarter and I would knock them out from my flat. I told him that wasn't going to happen, knowing that would be enough for Badwitch to get me out. Renny said he couldn't do it at his nan's either.

Renny and me toyed with the idea of dealing off the Ridgeway, but even though people were pretty sound on the Farm, there was bound to be some nosy cunt around who'd grass us up.

In the end, it was down to me. I suggested we deliver. It was the only way.

Renny would serve up his mates, take the money, and I could do mine, keep the money, and that's how it began.

On Monday evening straight after work, I met Renny at the Green, Green, Greenhouse, as we had christened it, loaded up with a bag of eights and set off.

Tank, Paranoid John, Hippy John, Chris Almond, Carol Basher's sister, Mucus, Gobber, Viv and Astrid all wanted some.

I didn't really think of myself as a dealer because I was selling to my mates. If I had been a dealer, knocking it out to strangers, it would've have been a lot easier. I could have delivered, scooped the cash and been underway.

Not with my mates though, they'd open the door, see me standing there. They'd be over the moon and offer me in for a cup of tea and of course, a smoke.

I had never seen people so happy to see me before, it was mad. The blokes would be positively beaming and if their girlfriends were there, they'd give me a hug and the blokes would stand back, grinning. They wouldn't mind. Everyone had their own way of smoking their green which I had to indulge in - when in Rome. I did bongs, buckets, hot knives, pipes, hookahs and of course many, many, spliffs.

A couple of weeks of this combined with working on the dig began to get to me, it was getting into my system, and I was feeling lethargic. For me weed would usually have three stages. First, I'd get the giggles, then I'd chill out, then I'd zone out. I was finding I was zoning out from the very first puff like I was a one spliff Cliff.

People didn't seem to mind though; everyone was affected in a different way. Most people probably didn't even notice, they were too busy doing their own thing.

I needed a break, needed it soon as possible, so when I found out Cerys was coming home that coming Saturday, I thought it was the perfect time. Renny wasn't too happy about it, but it would be me who was losing money not him. I couldn't have cared less, I had made more money in two weeks selling to my mates than I'd been paid working for the Manpower Services, and more importantly, I wanted to be fresh when I saw Cerys. We need to talk; we'd reached critical mass.

On Friday, the night before Cerys's return, I only took four-eighths out. One each for Coops, Mal, and Doggy in the village, and one for Whiff.

I would drop Whiff's off on the way back to Hertford. Mal and Coops lived with their mums and dads, as Doggy did, so it was in and out with them.

I planned to be at Whiff's by 8pm; we'd have a quick chat and a smoke, then I'd head back to the Farm early to get some much-needed sleep. It was the perfect plan, or so I thought, but when I got to Doggy's, his parents had gone away for the week and he insisted I come in for a few bongs. It was an offer I couldn't refuse, so in I went - I needed to make sure he was keeping quiet about our herb heist.

Doggy seemed to be enjoying his new role as an outlaw; didn't seem too concerned about the shotgun-waving interbred in the cab. It was good to see him confident, happy, but I knew once his mum came home, he'd probably fall apart again.

One good bong led to another, and the time passed in no time. By the time I left the village, it was 11pm. I was late. I was always fucking late. I was so knackered that as I approached the bypass junction just outside the village, I almost took the right turn that would take me back to the Farm. Whiff was a mate though, he was expecting me, so I carried on down the A10 towards Ware.

Whiffs place was only a ten-minute drive from Doggy's, so I was soon parking up outside the house on Milton Road.

I exhaled deeply, scraping my hand back over my groggy head, like I was trying to get my brain to spark. It was no good. I was wasted, but I was here now.

I'll chuck him his and get moving again, I can still be in bed by twelve at the latest, I thought, as I walked up his steep drive.

Knocking the door, I waited. No answer. Another knock, no answer.

Nice one, I thought, edging back down the drive only to see the door crack open.

I heard a nervous, "Hello?"

It was Whiff's mum.

"Oh hello, Mrs Hammersmith is Wh- Paul in?" I enquired edging up again.

"Yes, but it's very late, Brian's going to bed soon," she informed me.

"Skinner?" Whiff's voice echoed downstairs, "Come up, come on."

I pinned a smile onto my face and Judy opened the door fully, letting me in.

"Oooh, it's cold isn't it Mick?" she stated, shivering a bit for effect.

"Yeah, winter's on the way," I agreed, as I carefully took the stairs.

Once in Whiff's room, I pulled my last delivery of the day out, placed it on his bed, and took my usual seat opposite after moving a stack of vinyl. I noticed the album on the top was by Kiss. I thought, oh fuck, I hope he doesn't put that on again.

Whiff handed over my fifteen quid. "Skinner, where have you been? I was supposed to be meeting Shammy in the Angel," he said testily.

I picked the green back up, placed it in his hands, thinking, it's a thankless task this herb business.

"Shammy will be wondering where I was," he kept on. "Cheers for this, looks good," he acquiesced, rolling the package in his hand.

"I'm sorry mate, I was doing bongs with Doggy, I'm mashed," I told him, with a lopsided grin, creasing my face from ear to ear.

Whiff smirked. "Why do you hang around with him Mr. Baker?"

"Oh, he's alright. Believe it or not, he helped me half-inch this weed. We did a commando raid on this bloke's greenhouse. Got away with a load of plants."

Whiff began putting the skins together. "Loads of plants?" he queried, raising his eyebrows.

"Well, yeah, it was six… they were massive though, six footers."

Whiff eyed me. "So, what's this commando raid then?"

I had told Whiff about Sulli not wanting to join us, but I hadn't told him about the raid, I hadn't told anyone about the raid. Now to make Doggy look OK, I had told him. I thought, oh fuck it. I may as well tell him the full story.

"Doggy told me and my mate Renny from the Farm that he knew where this geezer grows his weed, and we…"

"What geezer?" he asked.

"Savy, you remember? Anyway, we drove down..."

"Is he the guitarist in Savage Circle?" he enquired, cutting across me again.

"What? Yeah, yeah, that's him, the mouthy little twat. Anyway, so we found this place, it's out in the sticks near Great Hormead, and we cased the place out…"

"Is he the one your mate punched?"

I exhaled deeply as my enthusiasm for the story wilted. I couldn't be arsed with this. Whiff wasn't big on stories, but I began to think there was more to this weird cross-examination. Was he taking the piss? Did he think I was bullshitting, or was he just not interested? Nah, we robbed the plants, it was a good story. Then I thought, maybe he's pissed off with me because he'd missed his night in the pub.

"Yeah, Renny decked him, but listen, we crept up to the..."

"Hold on, I've got some lager, do you want a bit?" he asked, grabbing a couple of mugs and pouring it before I could answer.

"Yeah, so we nicked this weed," I concluded, killing the story dead.

Whiff smirked, passed me a mug and then the spliff, and I took a couple of lazy pulls and started zoning out.

"You should come down the Angel, it was a great laugh last night," Whiff enthused, then cracked up laughing. "I was well pissed up."

I smiled, dragging my eyes away from his Slayer 'Hell Awaits' poster over his shoulder and nodding half-heartedly in his direction.

"There's this old boy down there, Stanley, he's in his fifties. He's a right laugh, loves a drink," said Whiff, creasing up again.

I smiled, didn't laugh, I didn't know what was so funny.

He stared at me. Confusion etched its way across his face.

I passed him the spliff. "What was he saying then?" I asked, trying to find out what was so funny.

Whiff took it. "No, no, it was the way he kept coming out with stuff," he said, descending into more fits of laughter.

"Nice one."

Whiff smirked, shaking his head. "You've lost the vibe Skinner."

I thought, if he fucking smirks at me again, I'm going to smack him one. I've had enough of this bullshit. OK, so I was a bit late, alright, really late, so what? I've put myself out to deliver him his green and this is what I get.

No. No. No. I told myself to shut up, I was knackered out, zoned out. If I sit here for another twenty minutes or so listening to him wittering on about what a great laugh he had in the pub, I can say, 'OK mate, I've got to get a move on'. I can go home get some rest, regroup and everything will be fine. You never know, I might be able to persuade him not to go to university, to stay here and rebuild the band with me. I thought this can't get any worse.

Whiff reached forward, smirked at me, grabbed the Kiss album off the stack, and put it on his turntable.

I pleaded, "Come on man it's too late for that, your old man's coming up to bed soon," clutching at straws.

"Don't worry about them, they're OK. I know you don't like it, but this track is amazing."

The first time I heard Kiss, I was straight and thought they were shit. I was stoned now, more in tune with the music. Now I knew they were shit.

Whiff was bopping about, doing a bit of air guitar, chucking the lager down his throat, animatedly chatting about how pissed up he'd got with Custer the week before in the Get Punched Up House. I tried to nod and say 'Yeah' at the appropriate moments, but the truth was, I couldn't really hear what he was going on about. It seemed to be the same self-indulgent story repeated over and over again: 'I met so and so in some pub, and we got pissed and it was a great laugh.'

He soon noticed I wasn't nodding at the right moments. I'm sure he called me a twat under his breath a couple of times, but I couldn't be sure, I started thinking I was getting paranoid, but I'd seen him do it to other people on many occasions.

Whiff smirked at me, leant forwards and grabbed another record, dropping it onto the revolving deck. I stopped zoning out, hoping for something better, then put my mug to my lips to take a sip of lager.

'COCK-A-DOODLE-DOO' blared out of the speakers.

It was one of his BBC sound effects records.

Whiff creased up. "Some numb dumb plastic heads need to wake up," he drawled, eyeing me proactively.

"What?" I snarled, lowering my mug.

Whiff smirked, "Some miserable bastards have got nothing to say for themselves."

I smashed my mug up onto his chin.

His eyes bulged wide, and he fell backwards on his bed.

I stood over him. "You fucking wanker," I shouted into his petrified face and pounded out of the room and down the stairs.

Judy's head popped out of the lounge. "Is everything alright, Mick?"

I said nothing.

"Is Paul OK?"

"No, he's a fucking slag, Mrs Hammersmith."

I wrenched the door open and walked off into the darkness.

Chapter Six

Threesome's a Crowd

Cerys and me had a wonderful time on the weekends when my mum and dad left the village for a house-hunting trip to Cornwall. It was drink, eat, shag, repeat. We drank every drop of alcohol in the house, including my old man's bottle of mead. We cleared out the larder and fridge using every plate, knife, fork, and spoon in the kitchen, and most importantly shagged in every room of the house.

One Sunday morning, we even had a go at it in the garage, but my mum's friend Mrs Lynch, or 'Mrs Get Lynched' as we called her, the village gossip, came around and started nosing about near the up and over door.

I was about to flip the switch, so we were slowly revealed to her - give the stupid old bag a heart attack, but even though Cerys thought it was funny, she wouldn't let me go near it. During the week we were far more restrained, with the favoured three, or the 'DES' as we called it. Drinking. Eating. Shagging.

I was working as a roofer, while Cerys was finishing off her GCSEs at Turnford College, still following her dream of becoming a Registered General Nurse.

Cerys was not only working hard, she was meeting new people every day. One of them was Jackie Haze, who also wanted to be an RGN. Weirdly enough, she lived opposite my dig mate Tank, on Raynham Street in Hertford.

Jackie was a friendly girl with an infectious smile, so if I was in the area after work, I didn't mind picking her up and taking her home, before Cerys and me went back to Ducketts Wood to see if DES was about.

Once my mum and dad had found their idyllic home, or their 'coffin by the sea' as my old man cynically called it, and came back, our DES fun had to stop. If I was anywhere near Turnford, I would still give them a lift, though.

One day, I got up there early. It was cold and I was bored waiting for them to show, so I took a stroll around the campus and happened to come across their class. Peeping through the window into the classroom, I could see Cerys and Jackie sitting at the front, heads down, studiously jotting down notes.

I tapped on the door and bustled in, looking flustered, "Er, excuse me, sorry to disturb you but, is this the biology class?" I enquired, doing my best impression of a lost student.

Cerys was absolutely mortified - her face warned me of repercussions later on - while Jackie burst out laughing, putting her hand over her mouth and turning away.

"No, sorry, this is maths, Biology is usually in Block A," smiled the tutor at the poor lost soul. "What's your tutor's name?"

"OK Block A, right cheers," I confirmed, retreating fast.

I took one more look at the girls.

Cerys was cracking up now and although Jackie had her back to me, I could see her shoulders heaving, trying to hold it in.

Cerys told me that after my intrusion, she was always nervous in class when someone knocked on the door, expecting to see my gormless face grinning at her.

Even without our DES res, Cerys and me still had plenty of laughs. We went to gigs, we went out for meals, we went out with her new college mates and their boyfriends to drink in different pubs.

I started to fall in love with her and I thought she felt the same way, but things were soon on the turn.

Once she'd secured her place, a living-in place at Chase Farm Hospital in Enfield, she started to feel the pressure. It was like time slowed down for her.

Cerys changed; she seemed distracted, didn't seem to laugh so easily anymore. I tried to be supportive, but I had my own troubles too with my parents moving away. Sometimes, the pressure on us was unendurable and we ended up having arguments over trivialities. We'd be on the verge of splitting up, then one of us would see some sense, and pull us both back, and things would be good again.

Only a couple of weeks after my parents moved away, I waved goodbye to Cerys and my world came crashing down. I really believed it was over for us. Enfield may as well have been on the moon as far as I was concerned. After she'd settled in, though, I drove up and visited her in one of the nurse's homes.

Nothing had changed and I was so relieved, it was like DES res all over again. Better, even. Instead of cuddling up in bed all day, we spent most of the day in one of the NHS's huge baths in a lather or 'scrubbing each other down' as we called it.

Cerys settled in quickly and threw herself into her work and her social life. It was a totally different world again, but this time it was more full-on than college. There were shifts to work. Earlies, lates and the dreaded nights, all requiring new skills. On the social side, outside of work, there were new people to meet, new places to hang out, to see, and of course those notorious nurses' and doctors' parties.

I went to as many as I could, but I couldn't go to all of them, it was impossible. Sometimes they would just happen. It didn't bother me, though, I had plenty going on in Hertford.

Then one day during a phone call, Cerys casually told me she'd been dancing with some doctor at a party the night before, and he'd kissed her.

For her, it was nothing, a throwaway comment. There was nothing in it, they had been drunk after all. For me though, it felt like something. I tried to hide my anger, but Cerys knew me well enough by then and accused me of being jealous.

Fucking was I. One hundred per cent. Some poncy fucking doctor had not only put his hands on her, he had kissed her on the lips, the same lips that I kiss. I asked her how she would have felt if some girl kissed me, and she told me in no uncertain terms that she would have trusted me.

I knew then that I was in trouble. This wasn't just about some puckered-up wanker with clean hands and a stethoscope. It was about me; this was about trust. I didn't and couldn't trust anyone. It wasn't anything to do with being a punk, either. It was ingrained into me as a kid, and the kid is the father of the man.

In the end, she lost it. She'd had enough of my 'bullshit', and she slammed the phone down on me. I phoned back several times and got no reply, so I drove up to see her, and thankfully, we sorted it out.

I swore to myself that I would never do that again. Cerys was like me, a free spirit, if it had been the other way around, I would have been pissed off too.

I thought everything was back to normal after that, but when I phoned her to leave a message, her mate Natalie told me she was at a party when she'd told me she was on a late that night. I was livid, but I wanted to talk to her face to face to see her reaction, try to read her, find out what happened. If it did get out of hand, they'd be no hanging up on me this time. We'd sort it out then and there.

So the next day, I reined in my anger, called her up and asked her when she was coming home next. She said, 'next Saturday', and 'can we go to the Anchor' as she, 'wanted to see everybody again'. I'd said, 'No problem', but just as I was about to hang up, she asked what the matter was. I thought, oh fuck, I kept it cool though, telling her, 'Badwitch was up to her little tricks again,' and she believed me.

That was the week before. Now it was time to see where I stood.

I hadn't been in the Anchor for a long time, but as I flung open the heavy door, I doubted it had changed much. It would be the same lads, doing what they always did, getting pissed up and enjoying the moment. My eyes scanned the bar. It looked like some of them were in tonight. Lucy 'Flat' Chesterman, Ski Sunday, Mal, Coops, Ronnie, Lee, Glyn, Danny, Taddy, and Craig. Then over by the fruit machine, I spotted Dave and Phil, chatting, pints in hand. I went straight over.

"Dave... How you going, man? You OK Phil?"

"Skinner, weyyyy, long time no see," Dave greeted me, shaking my hand.

Phil grinned. "I'm not shaking the hand of a hypocrite," he said, mimicking the village vicar, Hilary Charman.

I cracked up. "How is the nutter these days?"

Phil cracked another grin. "Still a fruitcake… Snakebite, Skinner?" he asked, already knowing the answer. "You tell him, Dave," he said as he decanted to the bar.

Dave snorted and shook his head. "Oh my god, you're not going to believe this one. You know it was baking hot in July? Well, he was only down by the river, offering to baptise people's kids."

I fell about. "Nahhh, surely not?"

Dave took a sip of his pint, then put it on top of the fruit machine. "Yeah, he asked Ski Sunday if she'd like to have her little one Jade done, and she told him to fuck off."

"I'll tell you what, he should have asked her if she wanted a baptising," I said, throwing a glance at her cosying up to Danny.

Dave followed my look and slapped his forehead. "Ah dear, it's too late for her."

I cackled. "The whole of the sea of Galilee couldn't wash away her sins... Who's the dad then?"

"Nobody knows Skin, I don't even think she knows, she does look a bit like Phil though."

Phil bustled back over. "Here you go Skinner, one pint of snakebite, cheers mate."

Gratefully, I took it, then blew the froth off. "Cheers dad."

Phil froze. "What?" he said, glancing at Dave, who creased up.

"Oh, sod off, don't start with that again, I wouldn't touch her with a barge pole."

I smiled. "You should have said before you got my pint in Phil - you need to be careful with your money now, you'll need it for nappies," I advised him, sending us all into fits of laughter.

Dave sang, "Hush little baby don't say a word, Phil's going to buy you a mockingbird."

Phil placed his pint on top of the fruit machine next to Dave's. "Alright, alright, I'm going for a piss," he laughed.

Dave spun around all business-like. "So how did it go with Sulli then, Skinner?"

I shook my head and told him what happened. I also told him about the raid on the greenhouse. I thought I may as well, I'd told Whiff, and Dave didn't know many people outside of the village. Not anyone who would be interested, anyway.

Dave looked down. "So, it's just going to be the three of us then? The old threesome?"

I grimaced. "Er, no... We're more of a duo now."

"Oh Jesus, what happened Skin?"

"Whiff and me had an argument... I ended up smacking him with a teacup."

Dave snorted. "What?? You're joking?"

"No, I wish I was mate, he was doing my fucking my head in, you know how he can be sometimes? He was just... I reckon he'll probably go to uni now."

Dave grinned. "Yeah, well I don't blame him, after getting hit with a teacup. Fucking hell, Skin." He thought about it for a while, then burst into laughter. "Fucking hell Skin," he repeated.

"I think it's over mate," I said, scratching at my bristles.

"No, no, no, there's other bass players, isn't there?"

"Nah, it's over Dave, for the moment, anyway," I said, absently looking towards the opening door, seeing Cerys walk in.

Cerys looked amazing; she was wearing a ripped Animal Liberation Front T-shirt, a tight black skirt, and high boots. She beamed at me. I looked at Dave, and he nodded.

"OK, Skinner… I'll see you later mate. You've got my number, give me a bell, or come around my house."

I told him I would, thinking if I don't contact you, I'll never see you again, mate. It had always been like that. I never liked Dave coming up to my house because I was worried about what my old man would come out with. He could be really embarrassing sometimes, especially if he started going on about politics, but I didn't live with him anymore, didn't live in the village, so I couldn't just drop in now. I had my own things going on, and although it was nice to come back, the idea of whiling away my time in the village didn't appeal to me. I had done that.

"Cheers Dave, good luck mate," I told him and turned away.

"Hiya," said Cerys embracing me.

I whispered in her ear, "I've missed you, you look fantastic, how are you?"

She squeezed me. "Great, but I'd be better if I had a drink."

I let her go, playfully gave her curves the once over, and went to the bar.

Once I had got the drinks in, we made our way over to an empty snug, set our glasses down and caught up. I knew I had to ask her about the party at some stage, but now didn't seem the right moment; we were getting on so well. It was great to see her so relaxed and on form, she seemed so much more confident now she was out of the village. It really suited her. Suited both of us.

I started thinking I should leave it altogether, I didn't think I was strong enough, though. Something like that would always be a problem. It would gnaw away at me, drive me fucking mad. I needed to know - later though.

Cerys smiled. "It's nice to be back, isn't it?"

"Yeah, nothing changes though, does it?" I replied, giving the bar a cursory glance. All the regulars were in. It could have been four years ago.

"Yes, same old village… Oh, I met Del and Joyce earlier. They're having one in the Feathers, then they're coming over."

"They're not still arguing, are they?"

Cerys chuckled. "No, they seemed OK."

Cerys and me had been drinking with Del and Joyce since they had moved up from London and we'd had a good laugh with them to start with, but as their home life had got more and more chaotic, they had begun to get niggly with each other.

If they were going to join us tonight, I hoped they wouldn't be like that, because they used to bring us into it too. Not only was it fucking embarrassing, Cerys and me needed to make the most of our time together, and listening to a middle-aged couple trying to slay each other with barbed comments wasn't it.

A few rounds later, as the drink hit its mark, we were getting touchy-feely. I thought about asking her back to mine, so we could get even more touchy and even more feely. I wasn't worried about getting nicked for drunk driving either, as I could go the back way to mine, using Anchor Lane, then cut through Bengeo.

I couldn't think of a better way to end the night, so I ran my hand up the inside of her thigh, was just about to ask her when I heard Del's voice.

"You alright stranger? What you having then? Snakebite?" he shouted over.

"Del you alright man? Yeah, please," I said, removing my hand.

Joyce gave us a big friendly wave, nudging Del in the back.

The pair soon joined us in our snug, bringing a tray loaded with drinks with them.

Del carefully placed the tray on the table and grinned. "Hey Mick, what's worse than sweat on Olivia Newton John?" he asked.

"Oh, bloody hell Del, that's an old one, he's heard that one before, haven't you, Michael?" Joyce chided.

Cracking up I said, "Is the answer 'come on Eileen' by any chance?"

Joyce crowed. "See… You need to get some new jokes Del."

"Huh, I need to get a new wife more like," Del told me, rolling his eyes.

"Oh, don't bloody start Del."

"I'm not starting, I was just telling a joke, wasn't I, Mick?"

I stayed out of it and picked my pint up.

"Don't bring him into it," said Joyce, smiling at me.

"You just can't let anything go, can you?"

"Oh, shut up Del," she said, smirking at Cerys who, like me, didn't know what to say or where to look.

Cerys and me raised our eyebrows and let them get on with it, but after a little while it started getting to me. I thought Joyce was picking on him for nothing. He was only trying to have a laugh. Conversely, Cerys seemed to be on Joyce's side, ignoring Del and only chatting with her or me.

In the face of this united female front, Del seemed to have thrown the towel in, but Joyce still carried on probing his male insecurities for a while, looking for a reaction. She soon found what she was looking for when she started berating him about his DIY skills.

Del jumped up. "Fuck this, I'm going to the bog."

Joyce cackled, "Well, I hope it doesn't need painting, we won't see you for the next year... I'll get the drinks in, shall I?" she taunted his retreating frame.

Joyce drained her glass. "Be back in a minute."

As soon as she'd gone, I spun on Cerys. "Why are you being like that with Del?"

"What?" she said, shifting uncomfortably. "What is the matter with you? You were weird on the phone last week - and don't try and tell it was Badwitch. I know you, Mike."

"I don't want to talk about it."

"Listen Mike, if you've got a problem, you'd best tell me now, because I'm going back to Chase Farm on Sunday."

I thought, fuck it. "What was the party like last weekend, then, Cerys?"

Cerys genuinely looked puzzled.

I pressed on regardless. "Remember you told me you were on a night, then you went to a party?"

"Who told you that, was it Natalie?"

"Yeah," I confirmed victoriously.

"Oh, for god's sake Mike, not this again. Look they messed up my off duty, I wasn't on a night, so I went round to Rihanna's room and had a couple of drinks with her and two other girls. It wasn't a bloody party, OK?"

Suddenly, I felt fucking stupid, because I was fucking stupid. I looked down. I couldn't look her in the eye. Her hand searched out mine. "Look, Mike, I'm with you, can't you see that?"

I squeezed her hand. "I love you Cerys."

"I love you too Mike. Even though you drive me mad sometimes."

I creased up. "Yeah, well, we both do that. Come on, let's have another drink with Punch and Judy here, and then get out of here, yeah?"

"Yes, lets."

Del came back, then Joyce, settling another two rows of glasses on the table, and we got stuck in. I don't know why, perhaps it was the drink, but there seemed to be a truce between them. They started to be the couple they used to be, so when they asked us back to their place for a drink and a smoke, I thought, yeah why not? I'm way over the limit now. If I keep off the booze, have a little smoke around theirs, and leave around kicking out time, it'll be less likely that plod will be about as they'll all be down the Get Punched Up House, trying to stop the casuals fighting.

Del and Joyce's house was only a stone's throw from the pub. On a normal day, it would only take a minute to get there, but we were so smashed it took us ages. I was beginning to think that my plan to drive home was suicidal. In the past, when I'd got like this, I had crashed at both Cerys's and Del and Joyce's gaffs, so that was my new plan. Either would have been fine, but I would have preferred Del and Joyce's if Cerys stayed too, as I was as horny as a catholic priest in a creche.

Finally, we stumbled through the street door, into their sitting room, like we were four scarecrows out of the Wizard of Oz.

Once inside, Del grabbed his 'doings,' planted himself onto the settee, and began to build up one of his huge cone-like spliffs with his rolling mat, while Joyce disappeared into the kitchen to fix herself and Cerys a nightcap or two.

While I was checking out their mediocre record collection, a scream of anguish erupted from the kitchen

"Fucking hell. Did you switch the cooker off at the wall again?"

Joyce marched into the front room, chucking a smouldering tea towel at Del. "Del, for fucks sake, I put the cooker on and that was over the ring, look at it, it's burnt… You're going to burn this house down, you're bloody useless you are."

"Oh, do be quiet, calm down," Del told her casually as he sprinkled a bit of green between the rizla papers.

"Oh yeah, like I'm going to calm down… Would you be calm, Cerys?"

"Er, I don't know Joyce… I don't want to…." she stammered, looking to me for backup.

Del rolled his eyes at us both, "Why didn't you bloody well check it then? You stupid mare."

Joyce screamed, "Because I wasn't expecting some idiot to leave a tea towel on the cooker ring, that's bloody why." She began menacingly moving in on him.

Del stood up, facing her down, but she did not move a muscle. Her eyes steadily bore into him, daring him to say something else.

"Ah fuck this, I'm out of here," spat Del, storming to the door. "You're mad you are woman, fucking mad," he called and slammed it behind him.

Joyce exhaled and turned to us. "I'm really sorry, he's driving me around the bend, I think we're going to split up."

"Don't say that Joyce, you'll be OK," I consoled her.

She reached out and patted my knee firmly.

"Cheers Michael, you're one of the good ones. I really don't know what to do…"

Cerys snatched up her drink. "I do," she grinned.

Joyce creased up laughing, "Yeah, I've not seen you two in ages. Come on Cerys let's have a proper drink. And Michael, you get that spliff finished, I'll put the radio on. Yeah, yeah, yeah," she smiled and sang, "Come on, let's partyyyyy."

A few drinks and a huge spliff shared between Joyce and me had me zoning out. I sat deep in the settee watching Cerys and Joyce dancing around me. It was a beautiful thing; drinks in hand, they bopped about, laughing, pulling each other in close, throwing their long dark hair back. I couldn't stop smiling.

I'm not sure how long I was out for but when I woke up, Cerys was lying with her head across my thighs and Joyce's head was on my shoulder. I looked down Joyce's cleavage, she had a massive pair of tits. I looked up at her face and she smiled, moved forward and started kissing me. My hand found her tits and started kneading them, while my other hand crossed over and started on Cerys's.

Cerys moaned happily, then her eyes opened.

"What the? No way," she said groggily, pushing herself up. "I'm going."

I thought, shit, what have I done now, jumping up. "Hold on Cerys."

"Jesus Christ, I can't..." she said, raging now, opening the front door.

I followed her out in the street. "Cerys it was only a bit of... I thought you might be into it."

"You tell me you love me, then you do that. We're finished Mike."

"It didn't mean anything." I pleaded.

"Fuck off," she screamed, disappearing onto Youngsbury Lane.

I thought, brilliant, nice one, Mick, you're a fucking genius. You've lost your parents, and you lost your best mate last night. I doubt you'll ever see Dave again, and now after all the time you spent chasing her, you've lost Cerys too. It's a clean sweep. Bingo. Full House. It's a fucking Bullseye.

I snorted, totally fed up with myself, and went back into the house to get my jacket, only to find Joyce at the bottom of the stairs in her nightgown. She dropped it to the floor. Suddenly, I didn't care. I almost ran over to her, and we started kissing.

"Come on let's go upstairs," she said, taking my hand. I followed her up, stopping just inside her bedroom. I was mesmerised.

In the corner of her bedroom, a lava lamp emitted a rich warm red glow.

Joyce sat down on the bed. "Take off your clothes," she demanded.

I didn't hang about; I almost ripped them off and chucked them on the floor.

I thought she looked like a goddess.

"Come on," she said, opening her arms.

I walked over to her, and she took my cock in her mouth, working gently with her lips.

As she picked up speed, her mouth started making a strange plopping sound.

Plop, plop, plop, plop.

Downstairs a door slammed, then heavy footsteps on the stairs. I pulled out, ran to the wall between the door and the wardrobe and pulled the door around me.

Del stopped at the door. "I'm sorry Joyce, I'll be a better husband to you from now on," he panted. "You look like a goddess."

"Come on," she said.

If my heart wasn't going fast enough, hearing that it went into overdrive. I thought, not only am I trapped, but there's some kind of fourth-dimension shit going on.

Plop, plop, plop, plop.

"Joyce, do that thing you do with your nails on my balls, aarrrrrhhhh."

I thought. I've got to get out of here.

Plop, plop, plop, plop.

There was a squeak from the bed.

"Del, let's put some music on."

Suddenly the room was full of 'Rock and Roll' by Led Zeppelin.

Joyce's voice rang out, "Oh yes, yes, go, go, GO ON, GO."

Is this some more fourth-dimensional shit? I thought.

Peeping around the door, I could see Del's red arse pumping away.

He groaned, "Awwrrahhhhh. Joyce… Aarrrwaahhh."

It was now or never.

I slipped around the door, urgently scanned the floor for my clothes. They were nowhere to be seen. Fuck knows where they were, and I had no time to look for them either. So, doubled up and naked, I ran out, ran downstairs, and started scanning the front room for something to put on.

Del's place didn't have a hall; their coats were stored near the back door. I began padding through the sitting room.

Upstairs the music stopped: a creak on the floorboards. I froze. Cocked my head.

"I'm sorry Joyce, I've been working too hard."

"Yeah, well that's the only hard thing you've done," she scoffed.

"Here we go again. Fuck this, I'm going downstairs to watch TV."

Grabbing the scorched tea towel off the settee, I tied it around me like a loin cloth. I stopped. My car keys were sticking out of the rolling matt on the coffee table.

I snorted, scooped them up and legged it out into the street.

One of the good things about living in a quiet sleepy village was that most of the time it was quiet, and the people were asleep.

I marched into the Feathers car park, thanking the lord it wasn't gay night in the Buttery, quickly climbed into my van, and got the fuck out of there.

Now the pressure was off, I relaxed and started to feel very drunk. I was fine though. Using all my willpower and my knowledge of Anchor Lane, I guided the ungainly Fiat Fiorino around the bends.

As I passed Debbie Lee's house near the junction to Tonwell, a jam sandwich pig car fell into line behind me.

Oh well, I thought, that's it, I've been lucky so far tonight, it was bound to run out eventually. Then, I thought, no. No, I fucking haven't. I've lost my girlfriend, I almost got caught by Mr Floppy trying to fuck his hot wife with some instant reject sex, and yeah, OK, the keys were pretty good, but the rest of it was shit. Yeah, that's it, Mick luck. Shit luck. Now I'm going to drive like I've never driven before. I'm not getting caught pissed up. I'm not getting caught wearing a tea towel.

I was on autopilot; my hands were staunch, moving without any thought. In my mind, it carried on. I was in turmoil. I repeated the mantra: not too slow, not too fast, everything is legal and above board. Not too slow, not too fast. Nothing to see here, just a hard worker going home after doing a hard day's work.

I exhaled a whole lungful when I saw the jam sandwich indicating right at the entrance to the Barnardo's home in Chapmore End. Then it peeled off leaving our two-vehicle convoy.

One of the bad boys must be acting up, I thought, god bless him.

I floored it, putting some distance between us.

A few minutes later, I was back on the Farm, parking up on Longwood Road.

Checking to see if the coast was clear, I creaked open the van door.

Thankfully, it was clear, there was nobody about. Grinning to myself, I casually wandered through the yards, taking in the Farm in the early hours of the morning.

I pointed my key towards the lock in the door at 34, and it fell inwards, to reveal Pete and Badwitch.

Both of them just stood there, gawking at me. Their heads slowly traversed as I shuffled my way around them.

The alcohol splashing around in my brain told me, only humour could save me now.

"Me Tarzan," I declared, pointing at my loin cloth. "You Jane, er Janine," I declared, pointing at Janine.

Pete and Badwitch continued to gawk.

I closed the door and buried my head in my hands.

Chapter Seven

Dirty Den Gets Clean

A couple of cups of inky tea with three sugars made me feel a lot better the next morning. So much so, that I decided to make another one. While I waited for the kettle to boil, Pete strolled in, a big grin plastered on his face.

"What happened to you last night?"

"It's a long story, Pete."

Pete guffawed. "I bet."

I told him what had happened, missing out the stuff about Cerys. I didn't want to air my dirty washing in public. I would phone her first, then if we were OK, I'd tell him. I didn't moan or whinge at people. It was totally alien to me.

Finishing up where him and Janine came in, Pete cracked up. "That's totally bonkers Skinner, we thought you'd been to a Toga party."

"Nah, the Romans didn't wear loincloths."

"Hmm, you could have been a Christian?" he proposed.

I chuckled, thinking, yeah, I saw two Venuses, then I was thrown to the lions. I'm lucky I've still got my loins.

Next to me, the phone rang. I flipped it up. "Hello?"

Renny was in my ear, telling me to 'be at the Green, Green at 2pm' and warning me not to be late, as he had somewhere to be.

I confirmed and hung up.

Pete cupped his chin, looking around furtively. "Er… Skinner, you do get a lot of phone calls, don't you?"

"Yeah, a few. We're trying to find a new singer for the band," I repeated my rehearsed response to this question.

"Righty, well someone left a message with me last night, that he wanted an eighth."

Oh, shit I thought. "Wrong number, was it?" I ventured.

"Only if there are two Skinners living on Sele Farm," he chortled. "Er, so… I was wondering… If you could get me a bit? My friends at college smoke it sometimes."

"What about Janine? She doesn't smoke, does she?" I asked incredulously.

"No. God no, definitely not. This would be between me and you…"

"I can do that, no problem," I said, thinking, that's the easiest delivery I'll make all week. Any week.

Pete beamed at me. "Brilliant, thank you."

Grabbing the boiling kettle, I poured it into my cup. "Pete, no hassle mate, but I wanted to ask you, has Janine got a problem with me?" I asked.

Pete fidgeted with a tea cloth on the worktop.

"Hmmm, well, it's not you she's got a problem with… Well, not really. It's more to do with her dad. You see, he bought this place for her, well, as an investment, and he's always telling her off about keeping it nice, he says she should…"

My mind sort of tuned out after that. It sounded like she was kicking down on me, because she was too scared to stand up for herself. Why the fuck couldn't she just stand up to her dad? Tell him to butt out, not kick down on me.

Nodding my head at the appropriate moments to show my deep empathy for his girlfriend, he continued, telling me, that her mum had problems with her migraines too. For fucks sake, he was going on so much, I thought he was going to tell me their loyal family dog had just been put down after contracting parvovirus.

Once he'd explained Janine's predicament in full, letting me know she was a good person, he gave me £20 for the weed, instead of the usual £15. As I charged him an extra £5 landlord service charge, including associated listening fees.

Pete smiled happily, "Cheers Skinner, can you drop it in later, when Janine's not about?" he said, as he disappeared upstairs and began whistling, 'Panic' by The Smiths.

"Sure mate, no problem."

I exhaled, took a deep breath, then picked up the phone, rang Cerys, and waited as the connections were made. Then finally the dial tone.

"Hello, Ware 3521," announced Cerys's stepdad, John.

"Hi John, is Cerys there?"

"Oh, hello Michael, no I'm afraid she's not, she's gone back to Chase Farm. We thought she was going to be here this afternoon, but she went this morning."

"Oh right, OK, cheers, thanks," I said, thinking, that's not good, I've got to talk to her. I've got to talk to her now. We've had plenty of drunken rows in the past. It's all part of drinking with your partner. That and the wild sex, but the key was to make sure you made up as soon as possible afterwards.

I rang home 11 at Chase Farm, feeling it even more. The connection seemed to take longer this time but finally, I got through,

"Hello, Cerys?"

"No, it's Natalie… Oh yes, Skinner. Hold on, I'll just get her."

My heart was pounding and my breath became shallow. I thought, what the fuck am I going to say? I said everything I could say last night.

Cerys said 'Hi' coldly, telling me exactly what I needed to say.

"Are you OK Cerys? I tried to phone you at your mum's, why are you back there?"

Cerys sighed. "I'm fine, they messed up my off-duty again. I'm on a late today."

"Oh what, that's well out of order," I said, feeling real empathy, telling her I was on her side. "Cerys, I'm sorry about last night, I was only messing about… What can I say?"

Cerys sighed again, only a lot deeper this time, "Look, Mike, I haven't got time for this now. I've got to work… I'll phone you."

"OK, Cerys… I hope your shift goes OK," I said, and the line went dead.

I stood there, smiling like the Cheshire Cat who got the cream; got the whole fucking churn. Thinking, oh yes, Skinner, me old boy, I think you may have got away with this one. Ha, ha, maybe Mick luck isn't shit luck, after all.

Now all I needed to do was get my clothes back. It wasn't really the clothes that were important, even though my leather was like a second skin to me. It was my wallet with the hundred quid in it that I wanted. I had risked my liberty for that.

Renny had told me to meet him at two o'clock. It was half one now. It would take me thirty minutes to drive to Thundridge and back. In my world, I had plenty of time, and there was no time like the present.

Thrashing the bollocks off the poor Fiat Fiorino, I got there in ten minutes and parked up around the back of the Feathers.

Del and Joyce's place is only a stones throw from the Feathers so I was soon pounding on the door. I'll play this one by ear, I thought, Joyce isn't stupid, and now they're not pissed up they'll probably be in love again, playing happy families.

No reply. I pounded again, and again, and again. I was thinking of giving up, coming back later, when a sash window slid open above me, and a black bag came tumbling down. Dumbfounded, I stood watching it until it hit me full in the face.

"Now piss off," a voice hissed.

"Cheers, Joyce." I grinned up at the open window. Grabbing my gear, and not for the first time in the last twenty-four hours, I got the fuck out of there.

Renny was sitting in a deck chair outside the Green, Green when I showed up, a ginger and white cat rubbing around his legs.

"Where the fuck have you been Skinner? Can't you get anywhere on time?"

"I'm only fifteen minutes late mate, that's on time for me," I joked.

Renny scowled. "Yeah, yeah. Very good," he said, humourlessly.

"Who's this?" I wanted to know, going down onto my haunches, ignoring the miserable sod. "What's on his collar?"

The cat moved forward cautiously, took a sniff of my outstretched hand, then, finding nothing offensive, rubbed his chin on it.

"His name's Liam, don't know where he comes from, just showed up one day. He's always mooching around here… Listen…"

"Oh, yeah," I confirmed, reading his name tag. "No phone number?"

"No. No fucking phone number," he said, antagonistically. "Seriously, Skinner. Where have you been? I've been waiting. I need to get on, there's a party at Lenny the Lamp's tonight."

"Yeah, sorry about that man, I had to pick up my clothes from this Mrs Robinson in Thundridge."

Renny sat back, intrigued now, his anger draining away.

I filled him in, taking my time. He thought it was hilarious, but when I told him Cerys had said 'I haven't got time for this, I'll phone you,' he snorted and shook his head. "And you believe her?"

"Yeah," I told him, immediately beginning to have doubts.

"Fucking hell, Skinner, it sounds like 'don't call us we'll call you', 'the cheque's in the post' or, 'I promise I won't cum in your mouth'. She won't call you."

"Yeah, course she will," I insisted.

Renny smirked. "Bollocks."

"What the fuck do you know about girls?" I bristled.

Renny stopped smirking, scrutinised me with cold, dead shark eyes.

Oh no, I thought, I'm fucked now, but I still held his stare.

Renny cracked up. "Fucking Skinner," he declared, shaking his head slowly. "Calm down, Skinner… We'll see, won't we? And I'll show what I know about girls. Check the greenhouse," he said, standing up.

Nodding, I slid open the door, half expecting to get blindsided. Nothing happened, so I gazed inside, seeing the plants had little labels on them.

"What's this all about?" I asked, turning one of the little squares of white cardboard over. "Pauline Murray?"

"Yeah, I've christened them all… These are my girls."

Renny edged me out of the way and reeled them off as he went down the line.

"Siouxsie Sioux, Gaye Advert, Toyah Wilcox, Pauline Murray - you've already met - and my personal favourite, Beki Bondage… Oh, and that skanky one down the end is Nancy Spungen."

I thought, this is fucking brilliant. I had to applaud the bloke.

"Yeah, yeah, yeah, OK, OK, I've got to go, I'm late," he said, hurrying me out and locking the door behind us.

"Beki Bondage is a real beauty, isn't she?"

"Yes, she is… You coming tonight then?" he called back over his shoulder like it was an afterthought.

"Sounds good to me, see you later."

Instead of going back along Tudor Way, I took the shortcut past the garages home. Beki Bondage is his favourite. I thought, yeah mine too, well, her and Siouxsie. If I had to choose between those two, I'd choose a threesome every time. That would be amazing. One day I'll have a threesome. It's only a bit of fun. Cerys will phone me when she's ready. Fucking Renny, more like. He's on the wind-up…

Up ahead, I spotted Jason Brown disappearing between my block and the next.

***

In between the blocks of Sele Farm, the last hour of daylight diminished, while above me, the streetlights flickered awake, replacing it with their orange glow.

I only had one thing on my mind tonight: to get smashed. It had been a busy week; it was time to let go. The party was probably in full swing by now. OK, being late was a problem on the day-to-day but being late to a party was essential.

One shove on the boarded-up door and I wandered into a packed kitchen. Pushing my way through the pack, a big rocker tapped me on the shoulder.

"Oi, there's a queue mate," he called out, indicating with his head a long line of people standing around a table waiting for hot knives.

"Skinneerrrr," called Renny, from the front of the queue, putting his thumb up.

Hippy John took two red hot knives off the stove, picked up a small piece of black hash with one, then ground the two knives together under a cut in half plastic bottle that Renny was holding.

He took a lung full, held it down, then puffed a huge nimbus cloud into the hippy's grinning face, making the big rocker standing in front of me roar with laughter.

Renny ran around the table, up behind me. "That's my fourth circuit," he laughed, grabbing the wall to steady himself. "Good turnout tonight, Skinner, and Carrie's here, she's single again."

"Nice one mate, well, I hope you get back with her."

Renny snorted. "Get back with her?" he repeated, sarcastically. "I don't want to get back with her. I'm only after a fuck. You're such a romantic Skinner. It'll fuck you up mate, fuck you up like hot knives," he cackled rabidly.

"Nah, course it won't."

Renny lent forward. "Has she phoned you yet?"

"No, it's only been a few hours, she's on a late, she's probably just getting off now."

"I tell you, stay single, mate."

Hippy John tapped me on the shoulder and gave me the nod. I snatched the bottle from the now-wasted rocker's big paw and nodded back.

Knives sparked as they came together, then a swirling grey cloud filled the bottle. I took a massive lung full, dropped the bottle and ran around the table, where I emptied out my lungs in Paranoid John's face.

Paranoid John was a picture of serenity, a big smile creased his face between two long curtains of ginger brown hair.

"Arrrrhh," he said. "Reminds me of the time I did hot knives with Syd Barret… It was two days after my birthday, three weeks before I fell off Hammersmith Bridge, the week after we'd been to see Bowie at the Roundhouse, the same year I dated Mary Quant."

Renny appeared in front of us, eyes blazing red,

"Oh, shut up PJ, for god's sake."

Paranoid John giggled. "No, you don't understand, Mary Quant was a fashion guru, I met her after I'd seen the Stones in the park, the year I dropped acid in Carnaby Street with Rod Stewart, a month after 'Maggie May' went to number one, the week before I…"

"Ok maaaaaaaan, yeaaaaah right on," I mimicked him in his dopey hippy voice, flashing him the peace sign.

Paranoid John chuckled, flashing it back.

Renny grabbed my arm, a couple of beers off the side, and we weaved our way through the kitchen into the less packed-out sitting room.

Lou Reed's album 'Transformer' blasted out from a record player in one corner and in the other stood Tank, Pat and Viv.

I waved at them, and they grinned back at me lopsidedly. I reckoned they'd done a few circuits too.

Tank shouldered his way over. "Skinner, do you know how long it took me to get home from Wareside?" he asked, trying not to smile. "Two hours," he told me, without waiting for my answer.

Renny and me creased up.

"What was the bike like? Any good?" I enquired.

Tank laughed. "Two fucking hours, I asked the old bloke in the house if I could use his phone and he told me to piss off and slammed the door in my face, I reckon he thought I was a distraction…"

Suddenly, the lights went out and Lou Reed slowly died on the turntable.

A couple of people cheered, then the whole room joined in.

Robbo's voice rang out in the darkness, cutting through the cheers. "Trace… Tracey? Get the candles will you, the meter's fucked again."

A few moments later, the room slowly began to light up again.

Tank passed Renny a fat spliff. "You got any gigs coming up Renny?" he asked.

Renny took a puff, blew out a pungent white cloud. "I've got Mary, Mungo and Midge Murderers, Period Cake and the Death Fascinators coming up at the end of the month."

I fell about laughing. "Oh what, that's bullshit man, Mary, Mungo, and Midge Murderers! You made that up… That's like… Er, I don't know, Hectors House Hangman."

"Yeah, I've seen them too, they're pretty good," he said, grinning through another cloud.

I cracked up. "Is Kiki the frog on bass?"

Renny creased up laughing. "No, Kiki's on drums, Zsazsa plays bass."

"I knew you were taking the piss. Talking of taking the piss, I need one," I said, noticing PJ weaving his way through the bodies towards us.

Once I had swerved my way through the sitting room, I wandered out into the hall. Immediately, I smelt shit. Taking a few sniffs, I followed my nose to Hillsey's room. It was empty. The zookeeper and his pack of hounds were nowhere to be seen, but you could tell they had been there only just recently, as the stench was overwhelming. I blew air out through my nose, clearing it, carried on to the bog.

Inside the toilet, it was almost dark. An orange glow shining through the ripped curtains from the streetlights was the only illumination.

On the left, there was a flowery shower curtain, behind it the white PVC of the bath glinted.

I rippled the flowery curtain with my hand as I walked up to the toilet, unzipped, leant back and let it go, feeling the relief.

"ZZZZZzzzzzzz," came from behind the curtain.

I froze. "Hello?"

"ZZZZzzzzzz."

I zipped up and slowly drew the curtain back.

Dirty Den was lying fully clothed in an empty bath.

Stifling a laugh, I dropped the curtain, unzipped, pissed out another pint, then after zipping up for the second time, I carefully drew back the curtain again.

I took another look at sleeping beauty.

It had to be done, I couldn't resist it. It was time Dirty Den got clean. I turned the tap on and stood back watching as the water cascaded down onto his trainers, expecting him to wake up any moment, then we'd have a laugh about it.

"ZZZZZzzzzzzZZZZ."

He just carried on snoring though.

I snorted, left him to his clothed bath and returned to the front room to find that Renny, Tank and Paranoid John had claimed the settee. I took a beer from the outstretched hand of Renny and sat down next to Paranoid John, who was talking in hushed tones in the surrounding candlelight. It was like a rocker's séance.

"I saw the ghost of Jimi Hendrix on an acid trip once. It was the day after I had fallen off my motorbike, a week before my first date with Mary Quant, a year after the coming of flower power, ten years after 'Electric Ladyland' was…" he said, leaning back, throwing his head onto one of the candles.

Whooompth! His hair went up in flames.

"AAAaaaah," he yelled, jumping up, batting his head with his hand, spreading sparks all over the place.

I sprung up too, chucking my beer at the miniature inferno, but he turned his head, and it splashed over his face.

Renny tried the same, again, PJ turned.

"AAAaaaaaahh, aaaaAAAAhhh, I'm under attack, I'm under attack," he screamed, flapping his arms, like he was the last Dodo on an island of hungry pirates.

Viv shouted, "You're not under attack. Get to the toilet, use the shower, you berk," thrusting him towards the bog.

Paranoid John, cut through the throng of people, leaving sparks in his wake and disappeared into the hallway.

A few moments later there was an even more horrific scream.

Paranoid John, only smouldering now, came belting back into the sitting room, wailing, "Dirty Den's in the bath, he's tried to drown himself, it's like Jim Morrison all over again. I was with him the day before he died. It was the year before I went to live on a Kibbutz with Eric Idle…"

Oh, for fucks sake, you stupid hippy, I thought, and went over to him. Trying to calm him down, I took him into the hallway.

Suddenly there was a stampede of people from the kitchen.

"It's the old bill - leg it," the big rocker shouted, surging towards us.

Paranoid John grinned at me. "I was at Mick Jagger's flat when he got busted. It was just after we'd seen The Beatles, the year before I met Ronnie Wood, a week after I'd…"

"Oh, shut up, you wanker," I bellowed, pushing him into the path of the charging rocker.

Ducking into Hillsey's room, I took a step, then stopped, thinking, is the dog shit on the left side or the right side? Oh, fuck it, when in doubt, go left, what's the worst that can happen?

I sprinted to the window, thankfully shit free, flung the curtains back, and the room filled with orange light. Thrusting the window open, I planted my right foot onto the grass outside, then looked back.

A copper came racing into the room, shouted, "Oi, you! Stoppppp…" His voice trailing off as he skidded and went down in the shit.

Cackling like a maniac, I squeezed my body out of the window, and legged it around the block, coming out at the top of the Ridgeway.

Down the road, there was a meat wagon and two jam sandwiches - coppers everywhere. There was no way I could cross the Ridgeway onto Longwood Road without being seen, so I went up to the allotments to lie low for a while.

In the silence of the allotments, I sat down on the deckchair, took a spliff out of my leather jacket pocket, sparked it up, kicked back and felt something rub against my shin. It had to be Liam the allotment cat, I thought, and sure enough, when I reached down, there was the little fur ball.

He rubbed my hand while I stroked his sides, then, with the connection made, he sat back, washing a paw. I took a deep breath, watching the little fella as he preened himself, thinking back on the night.

I hoped none of my mates had been nicked, Renny especially. He'd already 'been behind the door' as he'd called it. With the way things were going with the Tories, people didn't get second chances. No matter how small it was, if you made a mistake, then you were rubbish as far as they were concerned, a menace to be kept away from their so-called civilised society.

Liam suddenly sat bolt upright, staring over my shoulder, then there was the sound of weight, human weight, on the fence behind me.

Getting up quickly, I went into the greenhouse and picked up Renny's psycho knife. Immediately I put it down again and picked up the rolling pin, thinking, I don't want to kill anyone, and marched back outside.

A silhouette rose up in front of me. "You alright Skinner? It's me, Jason."

"My football came over here earlier. You ain't seen it have you?" he said, moving in on me fast.

I smashed him over the head with the rolling pin. He went down like a bag of shit, then I gave him a couple of good digs with my DM's to make sure.

"What the fuck you doing here? What the fuck you doing here, eh?" I kicked him again, then grabbed his collar, lifting him off the ground.

"OK, OK I'm going," he bleated.

"Get the fuck out, get the fuck out, you cunt," I raged, and dragged him to the gate, like he was a bag of rubbish.

Hawklike, I watched him to see if he had any fight left in him. He had nothing. He was all over the place, he stumbled off like he was drunk. Then, with one final lurch forward, he disappeared around the back of the garages.

Not surprisingly, Liam had gone when I came back. I reached down under the deckchair, found the discarded spliff, put it in my mouth, but my hands were shaking so much that I couldn't light it. It was time to go home.

I felt like I wasn't safe anywhere tonight, so I locked the greenhouse and made my way back around the garages, keeping an eye out for Jason Brown. I didn't think he'd bother me again, not tonight anyway, the way he walked off I could almost see birds flying around his concussed head. That will teach him a lesson, I thought.

Footsteps up ahead had me thinking again, though, but it was only Dirty Den or for tonight, Clean Den. He sloshed up to me in his wet clothes and told me 'some bastard' had turned the taps on while he, 'was in the bath out of his nut on Jellies.' He'd been dreaming that he was at home with Rosie and the kids when he'd been woken up by PJ. Then the old bill had smashed the door in, and he'd escaped through the bathroom window. Like me, he was coming up to the allotments to lie low. I was still in shock about what I had done, I needed to tell somebody. Den probably wouldn't have been my first choice, not the hundredth, either, but there was nobody else about and one thing I knew about Den was, he wasn't a grass.

So, I told him what had happened with Jason Brown, the plants, the lot. It turned out that Den knew all about the plants. He said if Renny and me wanted to move them we could move them to his house on Star Street in Ware. Rosie, his missus, had gone; disappeared off the face of the earth after he'd kept showing up, begging her to take him back. Hillsey and his zoo were house-sitting for him while he lived with Aiden. Sounded like a good idea to me, I told him we'd think about it. Renny would make that decision.

Den and me strolled back to the top of the Ridgeway, to see what was what. It was like nothing had happened; the old bill had vanished. So, I told him 'I'll see you later', and went to find sanctuary in my block.

Closing the door behind me, I wandered into the hallway. I'd made it. I felt alright, maybe a bit lightheaded, certainly cottoned mouthed, so I went into the kitchen, and ran some water cold into my hands, splashed it onto my face. I exhaled completely emptying my lungs, smiled. It was absolutely silent, then beside me, the phone rang, making me jump. Oh what, I thought, crazily, is that Cerys?

Putting the receiver to my ear I said, "Hello?" tentatively.

"Skinner? You wanker." I heard, then the line went dead. I looked at the receiver questioningly, slowly putting it down, thinking, who the fuck was that? It's nearly two o'clock in the morning.

Janine marched into the kitchen and switched the strip light on, blinding me.

"I don't know what's going on Skinner, the phone has been ringing all night long, I need to get some sleep. It's Sunday night. Pete and I have got college tomorrow, can you please tell your friends to call at a more reasonable hour?"

"What? That wasn't a friend, I don't know who that was."

Janine took a deep breath, "Well, they're asking for you, they know who you are… and they've been saying some… things."

"What things? What are they saying?" I cried.

"All kinds of things. Not nice things. 'I'm a rent boy, I'll be around later, can you get me some smack?' Some want cannabis. One said, 'Is that Badwitch?'"

I nearly laughed. "Rent boy, smack? Come on Janine, that's obviously some crank caller… And the cannabis, and er, what was it? Badwitch?" I added quickly.

Janine glared at me, "Right, well, can you tell this 'crank caller' to stop please. I'm going to bed now, goodnight," she spat.

I waited for her bedroom door to shut, then I took the phone off the hook, thinking, fucking Tank, you got me there, this isn't over yet.

Chapter Eight

Dog Days

Saturday and Monday were only one day apart, but they were polar opposites as far as I was concerned. Saturday was a day to lie in, rest up, after a busy week working on the dig, whereas Monday was where the week started, the time you earned that Saturday. I couldn't have one without the other.

Once again it was time to earn that Saturday. I felt pretty good the morning after the party, maybe a bit hung over but certainly ready for the week ahead. That was what life was all about for me in the blocks of the Farm. I couldn't sit back waiting for my old man or my mum to help me out, and as for the social services, well, ok, I took from them when I was at home, but that was a mistake, a means to an end, a way of getting a bit of cash while the band took off. It hadn't happened for us, so now I wouldn't take the steam off their piss.

Need was an easy trap to fall into, waiting for a handout, but I was independent now. I had learned quickly that I needed nothing. Only an opportunity.

In front of me, I had a busy day; the dig was going to be tough. We needed to get rid of the spoil heap from the back of the Indian restaurant, as the owners had been complaining that it was encroaching on their car park. Before I went to work though, there was a much more pressing issue to sort out: the plants. I needed to see Renny, see what he thought about us moving the plants to Den's.

If he was cool with it, my thinking was, we could load the plants into my van, drive them to Den's place on Star Street, drop them off, then I could go on to work.

Renny answered the door, looking knackered out. It looked like he hadn't slept much, but there was no time for pleasantries, time was of the essence. So, I quickly filled him in, then he grabbed his coat and we got underway. As we approached the allotments it began to rain lightly, then it quickly turned torrential. It was falling in sheets, which was good news for us, as they'd be no nosy bastards about, wondering what two punk rockers were doing with those funny-looking plants.

Once we'd got the girls (that is: Siouxsie Sioux, Gaye Advert, Toyah Wilcox, Pauline Murray, Beki Bondage and the skanky Nancy Spungen, whose leaves were already going yellow), loaded up, I floored the van and we headed for Ware.

Renny crammed a roll-up between his bone-dry lips. "So, you smacked him with the rolling pin?" he asked, lighting up.

I chuckled, "Yeah, it was just like something off Tom and Jerry… BAM and he was seeing stars."

Renny started coughing. "Ahhhhhh, I feel rough, Jesus."

"You look done in mate, like you've been up all night."

"I was up all night. After the raid I went back to Carries' place, we had a good night together, no strings attached, just a bit of fun… I got my end away, I'm happy," he told me, palms up.

I snorted, "You make it sound functional, like you were having a shit."

Renny creased up laughing. "Fucking Skinner," he said, puffing out a smoke ring, enjoying his roll-up now.

"OK, say if you fancy a bit later, will you just go around there, 'Oh hi, Carrie do you fancy a fuck?'"

"No, but I don't need to, I'll be alright for a while now," he smiled.

I smiled back, shaking my head. "You know what? You're like one of those starving third world kids, you get chucked a biscuit and you're all smiles. Me, I'm like one of those fat American kids - I want burgers every fucking day."

Renny cracked a smile. "Nice fucking biscuit though," he laughed. "So... Has she phoned yet?"

"Nah mate," I said, keeping my voice even this time. "It's only been a day, there's plenty of time."

As I changed down gear, coming up to the level crossing in Ware, I thought it was time to change the subject. I knew Renny could wind me right up and getting wound up with Renny would only mean one thing: a punch-up I didn't want.

In fact, I was beginning to learn that getting wound up and showing people your weak spots, no matter what they were, was a mistake. A big mistake, especially, when the person winding you up could knock a bloke out with three punches.

"Good party, wasn't it? Well, while it lasted." I said, tactically withdrawing.

Renny nodded, accepting it. "I saw Paranoid John walking past my gaff this morning, you should see his Barnet Fair, fucking hell." He creased up at the image. "He's shaved off the singed bits, his hair's just a mass of clumps now," he crowed, pushing back in his seat, chest heaving.

I wrenched the handbrake up on the steep slope at the top of Amwell End, waiting for a moped to pass. As it got closer, I recognised the cutoff denim jacket, over the leather jacket. It looked like Tank. Tank, on a ped? I thought, no, it can't be, but as he buzzed past at about twenty miles an hour, he gave me a sheepish wave.

I cracked up laughing pointing at the huge rocker. He was so big it looked like the little ped was stuck up his arsehole. My laughter soon died though, when I thought of the crank calls, and my possible eviction. I ripped the handbrake up, flooring the accelerator and then from behind me, in the back of the van, there was a loud whooshing sound, a crash, and the plants slid out of the back.

"Oh. My. Fucking. God," I said, watching them rolling off down the hill.

Renny shouted, "Stop, fucking, stop," and grabbed the handbrake, bringing us to a halt. "What the fuck are you doing? We've got to get out of here, someone will get my number plate." I shouted back.

Renny pointed at me, "Don't you fucking go anywhere, Skinner. I'm going back for Beki," he bellowed, opening the door, vanishing into the torrential rain.

A car came up behind, tooting its horn aggressively. Checking the mirror, I saw a Vauxhall Cavalier with its nose right up the van's backside.

There was a muted 'Fuck off', then a cannabis plant flailed onto its front window.

Dropping my head into my hands, I thought, we're going to get nicked, we're going to get fucking niiiiiiicked.

A few seconds later one of the plants slid into the back, the back door slammed shut and Renny jumped into the front, yelling, "Drive, fucking drive!"

I didn't even look, just hit the accelerator and we shot out of the junction, across the bridge, turning right on Star Street.

"I saved Beki, I saved Beki," Renny gibbered, manically.

Once we got to Den's we sat in the van for a while, listening to the rain hammering on the van's roof, collecting our thoughts.

Finally, I shook my head, convinced now. "You are one mental bastard, you know that?"

"Yeah, a mental bastard with a cannabis plant," he told me, logically.

"Which one did you hit the car with?"

"Nancy Spungen, the skank," said Renny, sending us both into fits of laughter.

Renny hauled the door open, I followed suit, and we collected the precious Beki from the back, each taking one side of her pot. We carried her round the back of Den's place. I knocked the back door while Renny dragged Beki down to Den's greenhouse at the bottom of the garden. There was no answer, so I gave the door a push and it swept open. Straight away, I got the smell of dog shit, so I pegged my nose with my fingers and tentatively mooched in.

Inside the kitchen, it looked like a storeroom. It was full of brown boxes of varying shapes and sizes. Picking one up, turning it in my hand, I read, 'Cabbage Patch Kids.' I thought, what a load of crap, tossed it down. I picked up another one which read 'Swatch Watches', then next to that, 'Preppies.' I couldn't believe my eyes; the place was full of tat. Scrunchies, Rubik's cubes, fingerless lace gloves, neon headbands, then in the corner, I saw a box of Sony Walkmans.

Nice one, I thought, I've always wanted one of them, they're the dog's bollocks. Renny won't be fussing over his beloved Beki for much longer, so it's now or never. Never was for wankers. It was a no brainer. I sidled up, flipped the box open, grabbed one and stuck it in my leather jacket for safekeeping.

Once I had smoothed my jacket down, checking it wasn't sticking out, I strolled into the hallway and heard the TV blaring out from the sitting room at the end. I was thinking of calling out, but just like the kitchen, the hallway was full of boxes. It would have been stupid not to have a quick look. I dodged around a couple of towers, then stopped. Checking inside the nearest open box, I saw there were VHS videos inside, I leant forward and read 'Sekas Cruise', 'Mothers Wishes', and 'Big Black Delivery'. I stifled a laugh; I knew what kind of videos they were. Bluees. I'd seen all of them around Craigs' place back in the village, years ago.

Suddenly, a river of dogs surged out of the sitting room towards me, followed by a wasted Hillsey.

"Whoa, Skinner, what you doing here man?"

"Oh, alright Hillsey?" I said, patting the circle of friendly hounds. "Is Den about?"

"Nah man, come in, come in," he offered, scratching behind his ear. "Yeah, yeah, come in. Have a smoke. I'm watching a film. It's fucking brilliant."

Nodding at my generous host, I parted the sea of grey and brown dogs in front of me, and followed him into the sitting room.

On the TV, freeze-framed, there was a black bloke, dressed as a delivery boy, getting sucked off by a blonde woman.

"You know what, I've got to go to work mate," I told him, backing out.

"Nah, nah, nah, mate, yeah, you go mate I'm fine here, fine," he said, his half-closed eyes watching me backing away.

I had to stop at the door though, as one of the dogs was rubbing at my calves.

Looking down, I saw it was Stinky Terrier, so I gave him a gentle pat on the head, and he let out a friendly, "Yip, yip."

Hillsey sniggered, "He likes you, don't you, Stink?"

Stinky Terrier nuzzled my calves some more, he then rolled over onto his back, inviting me to scratch his tummy. Why not, I thought, so I reached down, working my nails into his hair. He stretched out, fully extended on the floor. He was having a whale of a time, until Renny appeared at the top of the hallway.

It was just like someone had flipped a switch. He growled, spun over and charged at him, baring his teeth.

Renny hurled a box of giant Scrunchies at him, dodged back into the kitchen, and slammed the door behind him. "Hillsey if you don't sort that fucking mutt out, I'm going to garrot it," he seethed from behind the door, which enraged the little terrier even more. He pogoed up and down biting at the door handle, trying to open it.

"I fucking mean it Hillsey, call that twat off or I'll shove a Rubik's cube up its cunting arse," Renny roared, kicking at the door.

Hillsey stumbled out of the sitting room, pointed and creased up laughing at the feisty terrier bouncing up and down, trying to bite the door. "Yeah, alright Renny, calm down mate. Stink, here boy," he called out, and job done, the little terrier strutted past me, back to the sitting room.

Hillsey whispered, "He's a good boy," closing the door.

"It's safe to come out now Renny," I taunted.

Renny edged the door open, checking to see if the coast was clear. It was, he raged, "Come on Skinner, let's get out of here before I kill that fucking mutt."

Renny walked up Den's garden path with me close behind. I hopped into the van expecting him to pile in too, but he just wrenched open the door and stood there.

"I'll see you back at the Farm yeah? Don't work too hard, will ya?" he grinned, wiping a rivulet of rain off his forehead.

"Where you going then? It's pissing with rain."

"Carrie lives up on King George Road, thought I'd drop in on her."

I cracked up laughing. "Ooooh, be careful mate, two fucks is a relationship."

"Bollocks," he chuckled, as he marched off into the deluge.

"Oi, Renny, don't you want a lift?" I bawled at his retreating frame.

"No, you're late enough already," he called over his shoulder.

I hadn't seen it rain so hard in years. When I pulled away, the wipers couldn't deal with the amount of water hitting the windscreen.

On the dashboard, the clock said it was twenty to nine. It was no more than a two-minute drive from Den's to the dig. Worked started at nine. I had twenty minutes; plenty of time, so I coasted to the top of Star Street, then at the roundabout I took the turning into the Saracen's Head car park, to wait for it to blow over.

Easing the Walkman out of my leather jacket, I flipped it over in my hand. It was beautiful, worth a few quid too, and there was a box full of them back at Dens'. Fuck it, I thought, may's well be hung for a sheep as a lamb, turning the engine over. Tentatively, I drove back through the downpour.

Parking at the top of the road, I stalked back down to Dens', nipped around the back and cracked the door open. I could hear grunting and groaning coming from the TV in the sitting room. It sounded like the delivery was still going on, so with the sounds of pain and ecstasy all around me, I tip-toed over to the box of Walkmans, pinged the lid open, took a couple out and ghosted back to the door.

I had one foot out of the door when a dog started barking. It didn't sound right though, so I craned my neck, listening. There was a deep moan and then more barking. It was coming from the fucking TV.

You sick bastard Hillsey, I thought, what are you watching? Time to go. I made my way outside, checking the rain. It was just the same.

Then through the cascading sheets of water, glinting out at the bottom of the garden I saw the greenhouse.

I knew how Renny was about his Beki, he wasn't going to give me any of her, I had no chance. I thought, he won't notice if I took a couple buds. So I paced my way down to the garden through the torrent and opened the greenhouse door.

I couldn't believe my eyes.

Stinky Terrier was lying stretched out on his back, legs in the air, dead to the world, with the debris of Beki scattered all over the place.

I slowly reached out, towards the tangled mess.

"Grrrrrrrrrrrrrrrrrrrr."

I hesitated.

Stinky Terrier's eyes were wide open, scrutinising my hand. It's only a fucking dog, I thought, so I moved in for my prize.

"GRRRRRRRRRRRRRR."

"OK, OK, you fucking bogey," I said, retreating to the door.

Stinky Terrier's eyes fluttered shut. He yawned contentedly and went back to sleep.

I creased up, thinking, the bloody thing, I don't want to be here when Renny shows up, in fact, fuck it, I don't want to be here when anyone shows up, so I pegged it back to the van and got moving.

Renny was right when it came to my timekeeping, but he would never know why I was late this morning. I walked into the crew hut late, weirdly enough, not as late as usual. It looked like there were plenty of other latecomers too. It was only Hugh, Munch, Kath'll, and Paranoid John. My eyes went back to Paranoid John. Renny was right about his hair, it looked like someone had styled it with a bar fire.

"Aaahh, Skinner nice of you to join us," said Hugh twiddling his moustache. "OK, people, obviously it would be unfeasible to work on the dig today… I'm afraid it looks more like a swimming pool than an archaeological dig, so we're going to the museum annexe today to do some pot washing."

Both Munch and Kath'll groaned.

"Yes quite, well, it's a boring job, but someone's got to do it," he sighed. "Right," he announced clapping his hands together. "I'll take you two groaners, Katherine and Munch in my car … And Skinner, if you would be so kind, can you take PJ?"

Oh shit, I thought, I'm not sure I can deal with his rambling, no, not rambling, more like pointless anecdotes, this morning. Fuck it, when I get in the van, I'm going blast him out with Voivod's album 'War and Pain', that'll keep him quiet.

I needn't have worried though, as apart from a cursory 'Morning Skinner' as he belted himself up in the van, he was totally silent. I pulled out onto Baldock Street and took a left, thinking, I'll go the back way to Hertford to burn up some time.

I rammed my copied cassette of the Voivod album into the player on the console and sat back listening to the spooky intro with its chains and heavy breathing, thinking, this is the best punk/metal crossover album I've ever heard. It's fucking mad, a benchmark for other bands to aspire to. It's mad that all these people I'm passing now will never hear it. I was wrong though, because in amongst the crowd, I saw Whiff making his way along Ware high street towards us.

Immediately, I pulled over, turned the player off and wound the window down. "Whiff?" I called.

He carried on walking.

"WHIFF?" I shouted now.

He stopped, half turning.

I said, "I'm sorry man, I just fucking lost it… Come on man you've got to admit it, it wasn't just me… We were both being out of order…"

Whiff nodded his head slightly. "Yeah… Suppose, Skin."

Behind me, a car tooted.

"Look, are you going to be about? I'll drop in sometime, yeah?"

"No Skin, I'm off to uni mate," he told me, frowning.

The car behind tooted again.

"Well, maybe when you come back?"

"Yeah, definitely Skin. Yeah, that would be good," he said nodding.

I put the van into gear and pulled away, waving out the window. "Good luck man, whatever you do. See ya."

"Yeah, see you Skinner, you too mate," he called out.

I thought, thank God for that, that's one of my mates back.

"I had a homosexual relationship once," said Paranoid John, stirring next to me.

"What? We're not fucking gay… Whiff's a good mate."

"Oh yes, I've sucked a cock before, I was trying to freak out Elton John… Little did I know at the time. It was just after my first acid trip in London, the year before I went to Kings College, six months after I streaked along Pall Mall, a week before I went ballooning with Roger Daltrey…"

"Sounds great PJ, yeah really cool man… Were you into motorbikes?"

"Did David Gilmour like Vol-au-vents? Of course, I was."

"Nice one… You see, there's a bloke I know in Wareside who's selling one," I told him, putting my foot on the brake and spinning the steering wheel.

Chapter Nine

Relics

Once I made it to the museum, I parked up in the alley next to the museum annexe, made sure my brand new boxed Walkmans were tucked away safely in the glove compartment and sauntered up to the doors, feeling great about my little entrepreneurial move.

Selling the two Walkmans would make me more money than I'd make working for a month in the annexe. It was easy money. I could get rid of them, no problem, and it would only take me an hour or so, tops. Doggy's one was getting old, so he would definitely have one, and the other would go to either Coops or Mal.

I booted the steel double doors a couple of times with my DM'S, stood back and waited for the museum's security guard, Morris Cross to open up.

Morris Cross, or 'Crossy' as he liked to be called, had twenty years of service in The Police Force behind him. Like a lot of ex-police, he was still a copper and always would be one. He used to boast to Hugh that he had a nose for policing, which translated to me as, if he was suspicious of someone, he'd fit them up.

Crossy's head appeared from behind the rippling steel. "Hello Skinner," he said, in his usual mild tone, "Wasn't you supposed to bring PJ over?" he asked, looking down the alley.

"I had to take him home... He wasn't feeling well."

"Huh, I bet. Didn't want to do a day's work more like. The lazy bastard," he declared.

"Nah, his barnet was playing up."

"His barnet, was it? Very good, go on then, in you go lad," he smirked, moving over a fraction so I could get past.

I hummed the intro to the Rambo movie, going for the door.

Once I had weaved around the broad shoulders of Crossy, I wandered through the milliard of different displays in Hertford Museum until I came to the annexe door, leant on it, and disappeared from Crossy's sight.

Inside the annexe, it was like a thousand different worlds coming together under one roof. It never ceased to amaze me. It was quite literally piled up to the ceiling with historical artefacts. Historical artefacts from all the ages of Britain.

Roman armour, Saxon helmets, Viking swords, Norman sculptures, medieval coins, every age you could think of going right up until WW2.

Day in, day out, as the different pieces of history arrived, they all had to be logged: where they were found, the date they were found and what age they had come from. Then they all needed to be cleaned, measured, weighed, and sometimes repaired too before they could be displayed in the museum.

It was a painstakingly laborious process, and with so much coming in, it was an impossible task to keep track of everything.

On annexe days in the past, I had often thought about taking a few bits, but what would I do with a Norman sword or a Saxon helmet? If I walked into any antique shop in Hertford with them, I'd be nicked while I was still waiting to be served. That was before I moved up to the Farm, though. the Farm had its own economy, its own group of entrepreneurs.

You could buy or sell anything up there if you knew where the marketplace was, and after what I'd seen this morning, I had a good idea.

"Oi Skinner!" a voice jolted me, from my thoughts of larceny. It was Tank.

He was sitting at the head of a long table, with Kath'll, Muncher, and the Hertford lot.

In front of them lay bags and bags of broken pots and plates, which they were scrubbing with toothbrushes, then dipping into a huge bowl of soapy water in the middle of the table.

I smiled at the big biker, threw him the V sign, strolled over, and got straight to it, telling them that there would be no more herb deliveries after the unfortunate incident that happened earlier this morning. For some, it was like I'd just told them their parents had died on a coach trip to Margate. They were crestfallen; I actually thought Hippy John was going to cry.

Then I took Tank to one side and asked him about the crank calls.

To start with he thought it was hilarious, but when I told him there was a chance I could be evicted, he stopped laughing, told me sincerely that it wasn't him, he wouldn't do that. You could never be

100% sure with Tank as he was a proper wind-up merchant but getting me evicted would have made him a right cunt. Tank wasn't a cunt, so despite my untrusting nature, I believed him.

With my business sorted out, it was time for a bit of work. Taking my place at the square table, I grabbed a bag marked 'Foxholes Hertford 1980, No.4577/c', broke the seal and poured out what must have been a thousand pieces of earthenware.

It looked like a big jigsaw puzzle, but unfortunately, I didn't have to put it together - at least that would have been interesting.

All I was required to do was scrub each individual piece with a toothbrush.

Before I did my first day of pot washing, I thought working in a shoe repair shop was boring, repairing shoes, then polishing shoes, or if the shoes didn't need repairing, then just polishing shoes. I knew nothing, pot washing was on a different plateau when it came to heights of boredom. It was boredom in its purest form.

Not only that, it was pointless too. As once the pieces had been scoured, they had all to be re-bagged again and then moved up to the top floor of the annexe in readiness for Hugh to log them, along with thousands of other items.

I was about halfway through my first bag, halfway through a daydream about me, Beki Bondage, Siouxsie Sioux and a couple of cans of squirty cream, when something whacked me on the shoulder.

Spinning around, I saw Tank brandishing a claymore. "I'll have my honour, sir," he told me gruffly.

I chuckled, "Sod off Tank, I can't be arsed mate."

"Then thou art a coward sir…" he said, turning away. "Who will fight me?" asked Tank, slowly sweeping the huge sword around the amused faces at the table. "Is there not a man within these walls who will fight me?"

Hippy John scraped back his chair and stood ostentatiously. "I shall Sir… And to hell you shall go." He took Kath'll's hand. "I shall do it for thine honour, fair maiden."

Kath'll swooned. "O sire, thine purest love is for thee! Be careful, O gallant knight."

Hippy John kissed her outstretched hand and bowed extravagantly. He then turned, selected a sword from the sword cupboard behind him, picked up the stool he was sitting on, spun it around like a shield and advanced on Tank.

Tank flailed at him twice, and twice Hippy John dodged the lethal weapon and slapped his sword onto Tank's thick torso, making him retreat.

"Hahahaha, come on, O pagan galoot, come and meet thine maker. It is I who shall have satisfaction," said Hippy John.

Tank took a deep breath, drew the claymore back and charged, screaming, "Dieeeeee, heeeeeeeaven spaaaaaaaaaawn."

Hippy John thrust his stool shield upwards and Tank brought the claymore to bear down onto the stool where it exploded into a million splinters.

Pat stood up. "Bloody hell, steady on lads," he scolded.

It was too late; they were at the Battle of Edington now.

Tank swung, Hippy John parried. Tank swung again and so did Hippy John, their swords clanked together. On the second swing, their swords crashed violently together, so hard that a shard broke off and span towards us, making us duck.

Suddenly the annexe door flew open. It was Hugh.

He cracked up laughing, then remembered he was the one in authority. "Crikey. Stop, stop, people. Oh, my lord! They're very valuable swords - put them down," he chided, but you could still tell he was laughing inside.

Crossy appeared behind him. "What's going on here then?"

"It's OK Morris I'm dealing with this…"

"Huh, yeah, so I see."

Hugh reddened in embarrassment. "Now you two put those swords down and get back to work," he commanded, putting his tough voice on.

Crossy shook his head. "That'll do it then," he said sarcastically to no one in particular, and stalked off.

Hugh was a nice bloke, but he couldn't do tough, so when he launched into one of his 'don't mess with me' speeches, I dived back into the pot washing.

Once he'd finished dressing down the two noblemen, he told us he was going over to the dig in Ware to check on a few things. Yeah, I thought, I bet you are, you've probably had enough of sitting in the upstairs toilet reading the newspaper.

I smiled to myself. It was the news I'd been waiting for. With Hugh out of the way, it meant I'd only have Crossy to worry about if I nicked a few bits.

Crossy was a suspicious bastard, though, so wandering past his desk with a haul of valuable swords shoved inside my jacket wouldn't work.

Den's mate, Aiden, had tried it just after I'd started my first dig. His plan had been simple. He had put a sword inside each of his trouser legs, a couple up his sleeves and tried to walk out while Den diverted Crossy's attention.

Crossy knew something was amiss when Den started up a conversation with him about his illustrious career as a policeman. He knew we all hated police, and he had become extra vigilant. So when Aiden had clanked past him stiffly like the Tin Man from the Wizard of Oz, it was an easy cop for him.

I knew what I had to do; all I needed was a little bit of time and a little bit of luck. I had thought it through every time I'd worked there.

Pot washing duties carried on until midday, then Tank, Pat and me left the annexe for a liquid lunch in the White Horse, just around the corner.

I knocked back a pint then I left them to it, telling them I wanted to go to Tracks Records. They were a bit surprised, but they were more interested in their next pints than what I was doing.

I wandered back to the alley, carefully positioned one of the huge industrial wheelie bins at the back of the Italian restaurant opposite and nonchalantly strolled back into the building.

Crossy was having his sandwich and reading his newspaper when I idled in.

His head bobbed up. "You're keen lad," he grinned.

I laughed. "I only had enough money for a pint - thought I'd come back here, keep dry."

He rolled his eyes. "Go on then, off you go lad."

Smiling a shit-eating grin at the knob end, I nodded and strolled past him.

Once I was out of his sight, I legged it over to the sword cupboard, grabbed as many as I could carry and ran upstairs to the second-floor toilet. It stunk of roll-ups inside, so my assumption that Hugh had been holed up in there was right.

Moving quickly to the window, I gave it a shove. It cracked open an inch before it caught on one of its iron bars. All the windows in the annexe and museum had thick iron bars, but this one I knew to be loose.

Pressing my full body weight on it, I gave it another hard shove. Some plaster fell away, and it opened another inch. It was perfect. I looked down through the crack into the alley below, sighting my target. Again, it was perfect.

I fed the first sword through the gap and watched it spin once and drop right in the middle of the Italian restaurant's wheelie bin.

One after the other, I let them go and they disappeared into the coagulated food in the bin. When I let go of the last one, it twisted over and bounced off the wall, crashing down onto the concrete surface of the alley, making a hell of a racket.

Slowly, I put my eye to the gap.

Tank and Pat stood motionless at the top of the alley, gawking in the direction of the wheelie bin.

Oh please, fuck off, I thought, I'm nearly there now.

Pat stuck out a finger, said something to Tank's boggled face, and they marched up to the glinting sword.

Tank grinned and picked it up, beginning to swish it about like he was a nobleman again.

I wanted to shout out,

I couldn't. Someone might hear me.

"Oi Tank," I hissed down. "Taaaaannnnkkkk," I hissed some more.

Tank couldn't hear me and even if he had, he wouldn't have been able to see me. I resigned myself, there was nothing I could do. I just had to let it play out.

Finally, Pat realised the most important thing: the sword was valuable. Very valuable. He grabbed it off Tank, slipped it down the back of his neck like an elongated coat hanger, and pounded away from the astounded Tank.

Tank gawped at him, then finally, he caught on too.

I exhaled deeply, edged the window closed, took a piss, flushed, and made my way into the hallway at the top of the stairs.

Something made me stop.

I'm not sure what it was. An instinct - a feeling of something unknown close by.

In the dim light of the corridor at the top end, there were two rooms, one with artefacts from the Middle East, the other with European Second World War pieces.

Whatever it was, it was in one of those two rooms.

Tentatively, I ghosted forwards.

Now I was closer, it became a sound.

Breathy. Low. Guttural. Reverberating.

On tiptoes now, I slipped into the Middle Eastern artefacts room, dark shapes of dug-up relics loomed large all around me.

As my eyes grew accustomed to the dark, an other-worldly shape took form and in front of me, a long veil pumped inwards then outwards like a bellows.

I thought, what the fucking hell is that?

Then I heard Kath'll's voice: "Oh screw me you swine… Give me your mess."

I slapped my hand onto my forehead, thinking, for fucks sake not again - why me? I'll never be able to un-hear that, that's going to be with me forever.

If I get married, when the vicar says, 'Do you take this woman as your lawful wedded wife?' my mind will regurgitate 'screw me you swine, give me your mess.' If I have kids, the first time I hold my child in my grateful arms, my mind will throw up, 'screw me you swine, give me your mess.' My mum's funeral. My dad's funeral. I know how my mind works. I've got to get out of here before she says anything else to scar me for life.

In a moment, I was at the door, then out into the hallway, out of earshot and out of harm's way.

I breathed a sigh of relief.

"What are you doing up here lad?" raged Crossy, bouncing out of the World War Two room, arms outstretched.

He shoved me up against the wall, his face in mine, his chin jutting out. "I knew you were up to something coming back early, empty your pockets out," he bawled, spittle flying.

I smashed my arms up, knocking him backwards. "Get your fucking hands off me."

Crossy's eyes bulged, and he pointed. "What's in your pockets? Turn them out," he instructed, keeping his distance now.

"OK, I will, but don't fucking touch me again."

He nodded. "Come on then, get on with it, let me see your jacket."

I chucked it at him and watched the prat fruitlessly going through the pockets.

Once he'd gone through a couple of times, he handed it back to me.

"See you've got it all wrong… Rambo."

"You better watch your mouth, me laddo… I'm fully trained to break your…"

CRAAAAASSSHHHH.

Crossy froze. "Who's there?" he enquired nervously, looking into the darkness.

I stifled a laugh.

Crossy slowly swivelled to face the Middle Eastern room. "Come out now… I know there's someone in there…" his voice trembled. "Don't make me come in there and get you … I'm trained …I'm fully trained to …"

He spun back on me. "Who's in there, Skinner?" he demanded.

You don't want to know, I thought.

"You don't want to know," I told him.

"YES. I. RUDDY. WELL. DO… IF YOU DON'T COME OUT NOW, I'M GOING TO COME AND GET YOU," he shouted, still not moving.

A few tense moments passed, then finally, Hippy John and Kath'll sloped into the hallway looking dishevelled and sheepish.

On Kath'll's cheek there was a white globule. I thought, oh no, no, no. I won't be able to un-see that, either. 'Screw me you swine, give me your mess,' my mind chucked up just to prove myself right. I felt as sick as a very sick dog.

Crossy scrutinised her face for a while, shook his head unbelievingly, then began grilling them. "What are you two doing up here? Empty out your pockets," he demanded, while I took the opportunity to leave them to it.

Once I was downstairs, away from the new interrogation. I fast walked past a furtive-looking Tank and Pat at the door, giving them a nod, then ran at full pelt out of the main door and up to the wheelie bin. Panting now, I buried the swords in the bin's contents and slammed the lid shut, hoping it wasn't bin day.

That afternoon, I was quiet, conscientious, meticulous and boring as fuck: the model pot washer. Even though Tank superglued my toothbrush to the table twice, I managed to do twelve bags by the end of the day.

I was just tying up my last bag when Hugh came in through the museum door.

Hugh fiddled with his moustache. "Right people, I need to have a word with Katherine, Skinner and you, John," he announced pointing at the nervous Hippy.

"If the rest of you clean up, I'll see you tomorrow. I'll let you know if we'll be here or back in Ware."

Kath'll led the way with me and Hippy John in tow.

Suddenly I felt like I was back at school again; three naughty little kids on the way to the headmaster's office to get told off.

Hugh ushered us into a small room off the museum's main entrance, where we found Crossy sitting behind a desk, a determined look on his face.

Crossy leant forward. "What were you three doing upstairs?"

Hugh shifted awkwardly. "Well, we know what they were doing upstairs Morris."

Crossy frowned, looking puzzled.

I put my hand up. "What? I wasn't with them, I came up for a piss, heard something in the Middle East room, then Rambo here jumped me."

Crossy bounced up and came around the desk. "I warned you about that mouth lad."

"Piss off, you dildo," I taunted him.

Hugh blocked his way. "Right everyone, calm down."

Eyes bulging, Crossy seethed, "Ask him where he went after I found these two, he's stolen something and stashed it somewhere."

Oh shit, I thought.

Crossy pointed at me. "Give me the keys to your van," he said triumphantly.

Ha, ha you wanker, close but no cigar, I thought.

"OK," I said, handing them over to him with such confidence that he visibly deflated.

I strolled down behind the two mugs, then I started having my doubts. There were three nicked Sony Walkmans in the glove compartment, and this morning I had moved six, six-foot-high cannabis plants in the back.

It had fucking stank when I had parked up in the alley this morning, so much so, that I'd left the windows cracked open.

Not only that, when Renny had hoisted his beloved Beki back into the van there was every chance that a few bits of her might've dropped off. There was also that skanky Spungen plant dropping its yellow leaves to worry about too.

Crossy eyed me accusingly as he pressed home the keys. The door pinged open, and we were all hit with the pong.

"Bloody hell, it's like Bob Marley's tour bus. Let me tell you, young Skinner, if I find any illicit drugs in here. I'll be making a citizen's arrest."

"Oh, come now Morris, there's no need for that, we've all smoked a bit of wacky baccy in our time, haven't we?"

Crossy eyed Hugh now. "Huh, well I haven't."

Hugh moved uncomfortably.

Crossy sighed, shaking his head. "Can't believe anyone would want to smoke that stuff, it's a gateway drug, isn't it?" he lectured, ducking into the driver's seat well and inspecting under the seat.

Hugh and me shared a glance. This is going to take ages, I thought, maybe I should take a little wander around the back, check there's nothing incriminating in there.

I edged to the side of the van.

Hugh put his hand up. "Hold on Skinner, don't go anywhere."

You are such a hypocrite, Hughie boy. I thought, Viv buys weed from me for you and Tank told me when he went back to yours for an after-pub drink, he saw a claymore from Bannockburn above your fireplace in your lounge.

"Ah, ha, what have we got here," trumpeted Crossy.

Hugh leant in trying to see. "What is it, Morris? Is it those groats that went missing?"

Crossy triumphantly took the Walkmans out of the glove compartment, then handed them out, one by one to Hugh, counting as he went.

"One, two, three… What's all this then? Three Walkmans? You got six earholes?" he probed sarcastically, ignoring Hugh.

"Oh, leave it out, they're presents for my mates Morris… You know, mates? You know what they are?"

Crossy snorted. "We'll find something, Skinner, then you'll have plenty of new friends in the Borstal, close friends. Very close friends," he informed me, scrapping his hand backwards and forwards in the glove compartment.

After Crossy had completed his search of the front, he strolled around back, opened the doors and a stringy yellow cannabis leaf arced up in the air.

Crossly pounced like a kitten, making a grab for it, missed it, pounced again missed it, and it flopped down into a puddle.

"Hold up, there's more in here," stated Crossy, peering in.

I squinted in too. He was right, there were three spindly yellow leaves stuck to the side of the wheel arch.

Fucking skank Spungen, I thought, always let a punk down.

"I bet he's got a cannabis farm somewhere."

"Yeah, sure I have, I just used my cannabis combine harvester to cut it. All the plants are up on my weed farm, in wheat sheaves. No… Weed sheaves… Morris."

"I'm calling the police," he said, climbing out.

Hugh shook his head. "For god's sake Morris, we are not going to phone the police for three blinking cannabis leaves… Check the back, Morris, and let's all go home, this is silly."

Hugh and me stood back, watching Crossy search the van. When he'd finally finished, he disappeared into the museum without a backward turn.

Hugh shrugged his shoulders. "Right, well I'm sorry about that Skinner, but Morris is…"

"A wanker?" I ventured.

Hugh grinned and trudged off himself, leaving me on my own.

Breathing a deep sigh of relief, I piled into the van and drove away with the windows wound down. The stench was incredible.

I left it a few hours, then drove back into central Hertford and parked up behind the White Horse pub. Taking my suitcase with me, I ambled past the top of the alley, checking it out. Nobody was about. It was time to finish the job I'd started this morning. So, I strolled down to the wheelie bin and started dipping.

One after another I drew them out like a magician. Some of them were soaked in pasta sauce. Blood red, sticky; they looked like they'd just been used in a battle. Within a few minutes, there were twelve swords in my case. I zipped it up and strolled off, feeling like I'd just robbed the Bank of England.

Back on the Farm, it was all quiet too, so I parked up, grabbed the case and took it into the flat.

As I walked into the hallway, I saw Pete's Adidas trainers nipping up the stairs.

"You alright Pete?" I called.

No answer.

That's not good, I thought, I wonder if the crank caller's been ringing. Oh well, that can wait.

I hoisted the case up the stairs to the bathroom.

Gently placing the swords into the bath, I ran the taps until the bath was half full.

Now it looked even worse, the pasta sauce had turned the bath water crimson, making me feel like Jeffrey Dahmer cleaning up after a busy night.

Once they were clean, I towelled them off, cleaned out the case and took the lot into to my bedroom for a bit of fine-tuning. Separating the fanciest one with the least notches on the blade, I gave it a good polish with a bit of Silvo and held it up to the light. It was so beautiful, I actually began to feel guilty about taking it, then, I thought of my finances - or lack of them. I'd done well selling weed but now that was done. Now all I'd have coming in was what I earned. It was meagre, to say the least. I took home £65 a week. Paid £30 a week rent, plus bills. Food cost me £10. Baccy cost £5. If I went to a gig, I'd have nothing left by Wednesday. Fuck it, I thought, people say we should learn from history, well good for them, as for me, I'm going to earn from history and that starts tonight at Aiden's place.

I slid the sword down the back of my T-shirt into my trousers onto the gusset of my boxers, then pulled my leather over the top. Checked the mirror in my wardrobe. It was perfect. You couldn't tell it was there. Even when I walked down the stairs to the front door, my gait was almost normal.

Yanking open the door, I almost crapped myself.

Renny was standing on the doorstep,

"You alright Skinner? Robbo wants to see you," he informed me, not waiting for my reply.

"Later yeah. I'm going to Aiden's; I've got something for Den."

Renny snorted. "Fucking Skinner," he said to no one in particular. "Come on, let's walk."

"What's up with you?"

Renny shook his head. "So, what have you got for Den? Is it smack?"

I came to a halt and spun on him thinking, no, surely not. It's not you, is it, with the fucking phone calls?

Renny watched me closely. "Why are you going to Aiden's? You don't think you're going to sell stuff there, do you?" he cackled. "Tell me you're not."

"Yeah, I'm selling it to Den… All that gear down his place earlier on, thought I could make a few quid."

Renny slapped his forehead. "That's not Den's stuff, that's Robbo's. He heard the old bill were doing raids in Hertford, so he took them down there, keep them safe. Fucking hell Skinner…"

Instantly, it dawned on me why Robbo wanted to see me.

I had three Walkmans under my bed. Three Walkmans that belonged to him.

"Not that they were safe down there… Someone took twelve Walkmans," he stated, watching me very closely.

Here it is, I thought, if I deny that it was that many, he'll know it was me.

"Fucking hell, that's a lot of money, they must cost eighty quid each."

"More like a hundred and twenty… Robbo was fuming. Hillsey got a slap. A fucking big one. He was supposed to be watching them, the dumb cunt."

Renny and me carried onto the Ridgeway.

"Come on, this way," he insisted, turning towards Lenny the Lamp's place. My feet wanted to carry on to Aiden's, sale or no sale, but I had no choice.

"So, what you selling then?"

I sniffed, trying to sound cool. "I got an antique sword."

Renny chuckled. "Where?"

"It's here," I told him, slipping the handle out the top of my leather.

"Fuck, that looks pukka."

Renny thrust open the boarded-up door at Lenny's place and strutted into the kitchen. "Fucking old bill smashed the door in. Didn't find nothing. Then left it. There's kids living here," he spat. "Wait here, I'll get Robbo."

Drawing the sword out of my leather, I slapped a cut in half plastic bottle off a chair onto the filthy lino and sat down to wait.

A few minutes later, Robbo marched in followed by Shads and Brandon, then Renny. "Show Robbo what you got Skinner."

I sniffed again, got up and handed him the sword, handle first.

Robbo spun it in his hand. It gleamed under the single light bulb.

"Very nice, yeah, like it, can you get any more?"

"Don't know, maybe," I said, still playing it cool.

Robbo raised his eyebrows at Renny, handed me back the sword and walked out of the room, followed by the other two.

Renny's face reddened. "Fucking hell, Skinner, you can or you can't?"

I shrugged my shoulders.

"Don't play games with him, he'll hurt you, hurt you bad. You remember that kid Psychobilly I told you about? He had to leave the Farm because of Robbo… Come on let's get out of here… 'Maybe'? For fucks sake."

Renny shoved the boarded-up door aside, and fast-walked back out into the street, with me following close behind.

"What's up with you?"

"You're lucky Skinner… I vouched for you back there," he snapped, striding even further ahead. "There was only four people who could have nicked them Walkmans. Aiden, Den, Hillsey and you. I told Robbo you were with me all the time, but you weren't, were you? You had plenty of time."

Renny stopped and spun around, dossing me out.

"Listen, I don't care whether you had them or not, but if you want to fuck over Robbo, do it when I'm not around."

Nodding my head quickly I said, "OK, OK, OK, I get it. I'm not likely to, am I? I'm not stupid."

"I fucking hope not. Stupid is dangerous. Dangerous for everyone."

A couple of people appeared out of one of the blocks, and we walked in silence for a while. When they had passed, I said, "Cheers for vouching for me Renny, that's pretty cool man."

"Don't worry about it... Tell you what, if you give me the sword, I'll smooth it over with Robbo, see what I can get for it. Same if you get any others, alright?"

"Sounds good to me. If the money's good, it'll be worth nicking more," I told him, sliding out the sword and passing it to him.

Renny cracked a smile, spinning the glinting blade in his hands,

"Right you are then Skinner. This is good, I tell you, we'll do well out of this."

Nodding my head, we carried on in companionable silence, then when we got back on the Ridgeway I stopped. "So who you going to see this weekend? Infectious Haemorrhoids? The Spunk Bubbles or Thatcher's Ingrown Clitoris?"

Renny cracked up. "Nah I've got nothing on this weekend. I've got the Butthole Surfers and the Crumbsuckers at the end of the month."

I smiled, thinking, well, that's bullshit, another couple of made-up bands. "If you've got nothing on, I'm going to an anti-vivisection march on Saturday, I heard Conflict or Flux might show up, play a few tracks."

Renny paused, like he was thinking why didn't I know that? "Yeah alright, sound. See you later," he waved, turning right, heading back towards Tudor Way.

I strutted off in the other direction, feeling proud of myself, thinking about the craziness of the day. I had got away with some decent antiques, and now with a bit of help from my friend, I was going to get them sold. OK, he was going to take his cut, but that's how it works. If there's risk involved, then there must be a reward. A big risk for little reward wasn't going to do it for me, that's why I held some of the gear back. I knew if I gave up the whole lot I'd get less per sword. The way I played it, I was in control. I controlled the supply. If they had a buyer or buyers, then they'd have to come to me. It was supply and demand capitalism in its purest form; I had done the hard work, and it was me that was going to get most of the fucking money. I could be on for a couple of grand here, maybe more.

So deep in thought I was, I nearly walked past my front door. Sliding the key home, I popped the mortice and went into the kitchen to get a bit of grub.

This larceny is hungry work, I thought, smirking to myself.

I dug a couple of sausages out of the back of the freezer, put them under the grill, grabbed a bag of peas and started peeling some spuds for chips.

Next to me, the phone rang. My heart sawed. It's Cerys, I thought.

"Hello. Cerys?"

I heard a muffled laugh, then silence.

"Who the fuck is this?"

Nothing, no reply, but there was something phasing over the hum of the line.

It sounded like music.

I pressed the receiver tight to my ear, thinking yeah, it's music. It's punk rock. I know that guitar riff from somewhere. It's the Dead Kennedys, something off….

There was a scraping sound as the receiver moved. Someone shouted 'SKINNERRRR, FUCKING CUNT,' and the line went dead.

I jerked the receiver away from my ear, slammed it down, then picked it up again, leaving it off the hook, getting back to my food.

Suddenly, my day didn't seem so good. I had been on top of the world; Ronnie Biggs, the great robber, coasting. Now I was on my arse. If that had been Cerys

calling, I'd have been floating in the sky. She hadn't. She still hadn't. She said she would. Renny's words came back to me. The cheque's in the post. Don't call us, we'll call you. Nah it's only been a couple of days, I told myself.

What was that fucking music, though? It's driving me mad; I know it. I've heard it recently. I started trying to work the guitar riff out in my head. A, C#, A? Nah. A, C#, D? No, not that. I knew I'd work out, though.

It was only a matter of time.

Chapter Ten

Charles Dickens Machete Attack

On the Saturday morning of the anti-vivisection march in London, I woke up feeling tired, fatigued, like I hadn't slept well in days. My mind felt overloaded, overwhelmed and exhausted. No matter how I flipped it, tried to reason it away, it would come back, come back at the most inopportune moments. It was the not knowing that caused this incessant consternation. I hated this feeling.

Renny had told me Cerys wouldn't phone me back and now a week had passed. On Wednesday night I had given up the waiting game and decided to phone her to find out where I stand - if I stood at all - but Natalie her mate at home eleven told me she was working, she was on a late. Not easily put off, I had driven up and knocked on her door. No answer. It had been a complete waste of time. It was time to face facts: it was over. I thought, OK, I can accept that, but I couldn't accept the manner in which I'd been chucked. This silence had made it twenty times worse. Surely, I deserved better.

On the night that broke us, I had been drinking, had let the little head take over, then shared a kiss with Joyce. OK, things had got out of control when I'd gone back to get my jacket, really out of control, but she'd kissed a doctor at a hospital party. One of those notorious doctors' and nurses' parties. What had happened after that kiss? Did they go back to the nurse's home? Back to his? Who knew? Only her and that hand sanitised hand-job who kissed her.

I sighed, noticing my clock had stopped working, so I got out of bed, opening the window so I could hear the Farm coming to life. It must have been late; the early birds had stopped their dawn chorus and the kids were already out playing.

Hauling my duvet over me, I got back into bed and lay there, listening to their carefree shrieks of joy and laughter. It was life-affirming. Sounds of a brave new world, of individuals, untouched, before they are brought into line by education and changed beyond recognition. It was alright educating the kids, it had to be done, but why bury them in all the shite they'll never need and in the process reign in their natural talents? Some people were so educated, they were idiots.

I smirked to myself, thinking of that Sickos track 'Over Idiot Educated,' and there it was. That was the track playing in the background on that crank call. 'Over Idiot Educated.' I didn't recognise it because it was a different version. Probably Savage Circle's version. It wasn't Tank making the calls. It was one of those wankers in Savage Circle, and my money was on that mouthy cunt Savy. Mr. Jimmy, fucking Saville, himself. It was time to end this, end it now. It had gone to far.

Pete had been so fed up with the constant harassment that he'd been leaving the phone off the hook, day and night. When Janine's grandmother had been rushed to hospital with a suspected heart attack, her dad had called and got the engaged tone. In the end, he had driven to the flat to tell her.

Once she'd come back from hospital, she'd actually blamed me for leaving the phone off the hook. I denied it, but she didn't listen; instead, she stormed out telling me her father was looking into legal proceedings to get me out.

Pete apologised to me later on, told me not to worry about it. She was just upset with her granny being ill, and he'd soon smooth it over. He had also asked me for more weed, which surprised me, but not as much as his reaction when I told him I was done with it. He'd looked really pissed off.

I had seen that kind of love/hate your dealer thing in the past, but Pete was so angry, I thought I was going to have to punch the jumped-up little dickhead.

I shoved my duvet off and jumped up out of bed, quickly got dressed, marched downstairs to the kitchen, grabbed the phone and dialled Sulli's number.

"Hello?" sang his mum.

"Hi Mrs Sullivan, is Paul in?"

"Oh hello, is that you Jimmy?"

"Er, yeah…"

"I'll just fetch him," she trilled.

I suddenly had the urge to hang up, to have a cup of tea or something to eat and think carefully about what I was going to say. I thought, if I steam in, he'll hang up and the calls will carry on. It's time for a bit of diplomacy. I've got to tread carefully, I need to…

"You alright Savy? You're up early… Has Mia kicked you out again?" laughed Sulli.

I snorted. "Who's been fucking calling my number? Talking shit?" I raged.

"Skinner?"

"I want that cunt Savys' number now," I demanded.

Silence.

Well done, Mick, I thought, you really trod carefully there, he's going to hang up on you now.

"Skinner, look mate, I apologise, I didn't know he was doing it until yesterday. He reckons you and your mate, the one who hit Ray, stole his cannabis plants."

"When?"

"The night you came up."

"We went to a gig in Stortford that night."

"That's what I told him, he didn't believe me. Him and his mates have been trying to find out where you live, they've been to your village looking for you."

"Give me his phone number."

Silence again.

"Sulli, give me his phone number," I ordered.

"No, I can't, I'm not getting involved in this, I'm…"

"You already are involved," I cut across him. "You fucking string me along, tell me you'll join my band, then vanish and join this wanker's band."

"Huh, oh, I see, this is what it's really about? This isn't about a few silly phone calls… This is about me isn't it?" he replied tersely.

"No, it's about a cunt called Jimmy fucking Saville," I bellowed.

"Don't shout at me. I owe you nothing. Your band did some good gigs, then for some reason, you chucked your singer out. That's not my fucking fault."

"Yeah, whatever. You tell Savy to stop calling or he's fucking dead."

"I fucking well won't… It'll save your life, mate."

"WHAT?"

"You really have no idea who you're dealing with do you? You prick."

"Yeah, a bunch of Cambridge wankers. Remember I know where you live you posh fu -"

Click. The line went dead.

I slammed the phone down and did what I probably should have done before I phoned him - made myself some breakfast.

Oh well, that could have gone better, I thought, but maybe not though. If Sulli had been man enough to tell me he was joining another band, then none of this would have happened. I was always going to lose it with him, it just happened in a different way than I expected.

To be honest in some ways I felt better now, I felt purged. I knew where I stood, and I had told the person involved how I had felt about it. I couldn't ask for any more than that. However, it still didn't take away the fact that the calls would continue, but I couldn't do anything about that now. I had a march to go to.

I had just finished my breakfast when through the net curtains of the kitchen window, I saw Renny slouching through the yards towards my front door.

Oh shit, I thought, am I late again? Checking the clock on the cooker I saw it was only ten o'clock. It looked like the little hooligan was early.

I splashed a bit of water on my cup and plates, left them on the draining board and met Renny at the door.

"You ready then?" he asked.

"Yeah, let's get out of here," I returned, meaning it in more ways than one.

"This is going to be good, the last time I went to a march there was some proper aggro," said a grinning Renny, as he piled into the shotgun seat. "It was an anti-National Front march... NF cunts," he concluded.

I nodded, agreeing with his conclusion, started the engine and we got moving.

Whether Renny was coming along for the aggro, or he believed in the cause, I didn't know. For me, it was the cause, every time. Aggro for the sake of aggro was pointless. A lot of effort for little reward. Sometimes though, if you believe in something enough, you've got to fight for it. You can't be a sheep all your life.

Like a lot of punks, I had listened to bands like Conflict singing about our treatment of animals, but it wasn't until I worked on a battery hen farm that I really got it. It was cruel and barbaric, it was an affront to our so-called civilised society. From my short time working in the hen houses, I saw it was downright unsanitary too. It was a filthy business. Run for profit alone.

At the time I was surprised there hadn't been deaths from some of the so called 'products' being knocked out on the farm's production line. I had wanted to become a vegetarian then and there but living at home with mum and dad had made it impossible, so like a lot of people, I'd left it.

Once I had left home though, there was nothing stopping me, so it was a no-brainer. It was hard going to start with. I missed the simplicity of being an omnivore, but I soon adapted, thinking it of it as a small price to pay.

In the overall picture, it didn't really mean much, so I wanted to do more.

Cerys had told me about the Animal Liberation Front, told me how they marched not only for better conditions for the farm animals across the country but to stop the day-to-day torture of animals in laboratories too.

Vivisection, from the Latin live/cutting, the broadly used word for experimentation on living creatures made me feel sick. It was disgusting. Cerys had shown me pictures of animal experiments that were taking place right now in pharmaceutical companies near where we lived.

Pictures of cats and monkeys with electrodes rammed into their brains. Dogs in masks being forced to inhale hundreds of cigarettes a day. She'd told me it was all being done legally, for the benefit of humanity. In our name.

If that wasn't bad enough, there were the foul cosmetics companies dropping shampoos, perfumes, and all manner of chemicals into the eyes of rabbits just to make some rich old cow smell or look good.

I couldn't believe it.

Then there was the hypocrisy of the people who worked in these places, breeding all these creatures in the labs to be tortured, then, amazingly, they'd go home, curl up on their settees with their dogs and cats.

It made no sense. Talk about hypocritical, talk about heartless fucking bastards.

Cerys had played a big part in my involvement with the Animal Liberation movement, and although I didn't like the idea, it made me feel like I was going for the wrong reason because I hoped that she might be at the march today.

In the past, she had sold T-shirts on the ALF stall and collected money in buckets as the people walked past, but this was before she'd started her full-time training to be an RGN. I knew she'd been ignoring my calls, but I still thought I might be able to get her back, or at least get some kind of explanation.

"So has she phoned?" asked Renny, right on queue.

"No mate, I told you yesterday, it's over," I said. "How's Carrie then?" I shot back before he could comment.

"She's alright, we went to that Indian restaurant behind your dig."

I sniggered. Sounds like love to me."

"Telling you, it's just physical."

I shook my head, laughing. "If you say so, mate."

"I do," he said, patting down his combat jacket.

I smiled. "You'll be saying that at the altar soon."

Renny snorted. "Doubtful."

"Anyway Skinner, me old mucker, I've got some good news for you."

"Oh yeah?" I said, distracted, trying to keep my eyes on the rapidly building traffic.

"Robbo will give you £200 for the sword... He'll take everything you got."

"Nice one, cheers Renny. I should be able to get a few more," I replied, thinking fucking hell, my love life may be shit, but money just loves me. I could be on for two and a half here. Give it a few weeks and if I'm still working in the annexe, I'll be able to do it again - I could make a year's money in a couple of months.

"Yeah, he's really happy with that. He knows this dodgy antique dealer… Well, he'll tell you if he thinks you're ready."

"I'm ready when he is."

A car suddenly pulled out from the left. I slammed the brakes on, throwing Renny forward.

"Whoa Skinner, you stoned or something?"

"Fucking dickhead," I shouted, at the now crawling car in front.

"Nah, I just haven't driven in London before." I sniffed. "Hope you know where we're going."

Renny grinned. "Yeah, no sweat. I've got my trusty A to Z here," he said, patting his jacket. "We'll park on the other side of the water, walk up to the march from there. Before we do, I need to drop in on a mate."

Nodding slightly, I kept my eyes on the fast-changing road ahead. It was true I hadn't driven in London before, but I knew this road all too well. It was the A10. It went right through my old village to the middle of London. Many times, I had sat in the shotgun seat with my gypsy mate, Ashley, in his bright orange van, or in Dapper's red Alpha Romeo, the posh kid who lived in a mansion in Braughing, as they drove to the Frontline and back. Both had smoked a lot of weed when they had done it too. How they did it, I don't know. The traffic was total chaos.

Once we'd gone past Kingsland high road, I didn't know where we were, I was completely in the hands of Renny and his trusty A to Z.

"This is the City of London Skinner, where all the money is," revealed Renny, gesturing with his hands at the sky-high office blocks and old ornate buildings around us.

As I pulled up at a red light, I nodded, impressed by what I was seeing.

Renny pointed at the mostly grey suited office workers, swarming on the pavements around us. "And those Skinner are the city drones, the biggest bunch of shysters you'll ever see. They produce nothing, they just play people off against each other … They make millions out of cheating people."

"They don't look very happy," I said, surveying their pale faces.

"Nah they don't know how to be, they're living someone else's dream, they don't think for themselves … They're too scared, too scared to live. Think money's the key to everything. Sad bastards," he concluded.

From nowhere, a motorbike weaved its way around the back of the van and stopped in front of us, then another one appeared from the other side. Both riders were kitted out in harsh scorched leathers, both wore fluorescent bibs with company names with phone numbers.

I sat forward, squinted, and read, "GLH, Addison Lee," looking to Renny for an explanation.

"Despatch riders, watch them when the light goes green."

Red changed to amber, amber to green. The engines screamed and the bikes were off; they were racing each other.

Then another couple came speeding past us on each side, and they all disappeared suddenly into a group of black cabs.

Renny grinned. "They get paid per job. The faster they go, the more money they make. No tax, no NI. What you make you take. I know a bloke who did it. Did it for three years, made a lot of money, but he couldn't take the winters."

"That looks fucking brilliant, like something off Mad Max."

A couple more bikes rolled up next to us at the next set of lights, I checked them out again. Both bikes were raked-out old Honda CXs, kitted out with panniers and top boxes.

One of them looked like it had been chucked down the road a few times, its tank dented, its seat held together with gaffer tape.

Seconds later, the lights changed to amber. The drones crossing the road dwindled.

The two riders exchanged a knowing nod, hit their twist grips, revving their engines, then, as the light changed to green, they left us in a cloud of fumes.

"Fucking hell, I'd love to do that."

Renny nodded. "Yeah, looks like a right laugh, doesn't it?"

I checked the road we were on at the next set of traffic lights. The Minories, it was called, then looking further on, rising above the low-level office blocks, I saw the huge structure of Tower Bridge standing triumphantly, pointing up into a blue sky.

More bikes surrounded us, this time there must have been a dozen at least. I noticed the riders had radios hanging on their chests, some drawing them upwards to their mouths, shouting into them.

I smirked, "Watch this," leaning forward in my seat.

Engines revved, coughing out blue-grey fumes, then when the lights changed, I floored the van, and we were off with them, hammering down the Minories.

We passed the Tower of London on the left, then as we sped onto Tower Bridge the whole world seemed to open up.

I forgot the bikes; they were long gone anyway, now, my head was swivelling left then right. Right then left. I didn't know what to look at first.

To the left, there was a huge ship on the Thames. To the right Big Ben, the Post Office tower; all manner of structures old and new. Then above us, the metal, blue and white structure of the bridge scrolled over us. It was an incredible sight. I felt like I was at the centre of the world.

Not only are these riders getting paid to break the law, I thought, they are doing it in one of the most famous cities on the planet.

Renny hawked up a grolly and spat it out of the window. "Enough site seeing now Skinner, turn left here," he instructed me peering over his A to Z.

"Yeah that's it, Tooley Street."

"What? Yeah alright, did you see that?"

I spun the steering wheel, still in awe of the sights we had just passed, but Renny's demeanour told me it was time to concentrate, time to be ready. He sat forward in his seat steady, watchful, as we travelled through boarded-up warehouses, dilapidated crumbling buildings along a deeply rutted road.

If what I had just seen was the centre of the world, I thought, this is the opposite. All the opulence, the history, the wealth had vanished in a couple of spins of the steering wheel.

"Keep an eye out for the Dickens estate," he told me.

A couple of miles down the heavily pitted road, in amongst the derelict buildings, a dark concrete tower block rose up, then as we got closer to it, I saw it had a series of old tenement blocks surrounding it.

I pulled up on the main road next to the tower block as Renny had directed.

"I'm just dropping in on a mate, I might be a while… If you're hungry there's a shop over there," he said, pointing into the estate.

"Yeah right, cheers."

Oh great, I thought how long is a while? I'm here to march. If Cerys is there doing her stall, once the march starts, she'll join it and I'll have no chance of seeing her.

I stretched back in my seat for a while, watching a spider constructing its web to capture passing insects. It meticulously cast its silky thread between the sun visor and the driver's mirror over and over again. It was an amazing feat of ingenuity.

I was drawn away from the hypnotic spider by the wail of sirens.

A whole squadron of police vehicles raced past. Cars, bikes and about twenty meat wagons; I couldn't believe my eyes. I'd seen a few sniffing about on the Farm a few times, chasing shadows, but this was something else entirely.

It wasn't just your usual unfriendly neighbourhood policeman, this was a police force, an army, full of threat and menace.

A fly buzzed lazily in through my cracked open window and started to bounce off the windscreen, steadily moving towards the web.

In a moment, a sticky thread caught hold. The fly wriggled, spun, flapped its wings, fighting for its life, kept going until it had completely exhausted itself. Then with nothing left, the spider rushed out from behind the driver's mirror, smothering it.

For a moment, I thought someone was trying to tell me something. I told myself to shut up, it's just the way life is sometimes. It's probably the weed messing with my head. Or maybe, I'm just hungry.

Leaving the spider to embalm the fly, I threw open the door, stepped out, took a deep life-affirming breath, and ambled onto the estate.

It wasn't that different from the Farm, really. The tenement blocks on the Dickens estate were just older. Looking at them closely they seemed to be better built. They were definitely more solid than the Farm's blocks that were built in the sixties, using the cheapest materials that Hertfordshire County Council could buy.

Strolling into the sparsely stocked shop, I grabbed a solid Mars bar and a can of Coke, paid the Asian bloke behind his high counter, left the shop, and walked out onto an expanse of concrete flagstones.

Opening my can of coke, I watched most of it piss out of the top.

Suddenly there was a loud crash. Renny was running towards me, close behind him there was a big fat bloke in a white vest swinging a machete above his head.

"You fucking cunnnnntttt, get back here."

Renny shouted. "Leg it, Skinner, get back to the van."

He didn't have to tell me twice. I dropped what was left of the Coke on the deck, pissing even more foam out, and pelted off in the direction I had come from.

As I ran past the tower block, I took a peek over my shoulder.

Renny had vanished, but the fat bloke was still coming my way, at about half the speed now. Panting hard, out of breath, he had one hand on his chest.

He pointed the machete at me. "Oi you, you're fucking dead," he bawled, lurching toward me, his big belly sloping from side to side inside his vest.

I snorted. "Fuck off you fat cunt," I shouted back at the fat cunt, and tripped, ending up in a grazed heap on the concrete.

I rolled over and the fat bastard didn't seem to be moving so slowly now. He was moving like Sebastian fucking Coe.

His figure puffed up, looming over me like the tower blocks. "Punk, you are dead."

Smack.

Renny blindsided him and he paused, totally bewildered, like he didn't believe he'd been hit. Then he toppled sideways, going down hard on the concrete. He rolled over onto his back. Renny buried his heel into his face, and he was still.

Renny, calmly, came over to me. "Come on let's get back to the van… And don't run. People who run get chased," he said, strolling off like he was out for a Sunday walk.

Once we'd got back to the van, we piled in and I turned the engine over, putting it in first.

Then I stopped and stared.

Renny had a wad of notes the size of a house brick in his hand. He squeezed the lot into a brown envelope and quickly stashed it under his seat. "Wind your neck in Skinner … Are we going or what?"

"Yeah alright, keep your hair on, we're going," I told him, pulling away. "One of your mates, was it?" I enquired.

"No, not anymore."

Chapter Eleven

'Boots Scum Here We Come'

On the way to the march, I kept asking Renny questions, the main one being why had some fat Weeble cunt come at us with a fucking machete? His answer, like so many times before, was 'ask Robbo, he will tell you when he thinks you're ready'.

No way was I accepting that. It was bullshit. I had a wedge of cash in my van that you could knock a dog unconscious with. A wedge of cash that was obviously the proceeds of an illegal transaction. A wedge of cash that could see me joining Basher behind the door, and no one was telling me anything. I went on so much that he told me to pull over. I thought he was going to piss off, but he disappeared into a corner shop, returning a couple of minutes later with a pork pie and the NME. He got back in, raising it up like a drawbridge just as my old man used to.

"I want paying for this, it's my van, my risk."

"Give it a rest, will you?... I'll tell Robbo what you did, and he'll sort you out some readies, OK?"

"At last."

Nice one, I thought, I might not be in the know, but as long as I'm getting paid a few quid, I don't care. People say knowledge is power, they also say ignorance is bliss. In the grand scheme of things, they're both right, but if ignorance means I'll be getting paid, I don't want to know. I'll live in ignorance, counting my money.

Renny lowered the drawbridge. "You know you thought I was making up band names?"

I smirked. "What you mean like the Vagina Vol-au-Vents or Carbuncles are Go?"

"No, I mean, the Butthole Surfers and the Crumbsuckers, they're in here look," he insisted, pointing in the NME under the headline of new American rock bands.

I creased up. "For fucks sake. I thought Morbid Fridge was a shit name for a band."

"No, it's not the best name, is it?" he agreed, turning to the gig page. "Look at this, those posh wankers, Savage Circle, have got some gigs coming up… Fucking hell, they've got one at Cambridge Junction, headlining, they must have got some proper backing."

"Yeahhh?" I drawled, trying to push the green-eyed goblin down and failing miserably.

Renny cackled. "Big gig that Skinner." he taunted.

"Is it? Well... Good for them," the green-eyed goblin told him.

"I'm going, might ask Carrie. She was well into the Sickos.'"

"Oh great, nice one."

"You should come… If they're as good as the Sickos, it'll be a good night."

"I'm not going to give my money to those knob ends…" I spat, then hesitated. "You know what, maybe I should go up there, fuck it up for them."

"Maybe you should," he said, picking up his A to Z. "OK Skinner, take a right. We'll leave the van here and walk the rest… Westminster Bridge is just over there." he pointed.

Checking the street name, I saw we were on Leake Street, Borough of Lambeth. It was the same as Bermondsey here, maybe worse. Crumbling abandoned warehouses lined the rutted street, then at the top, near a section of dilapidated railway arches, there was a tower of three burnt-out cars.

I parked up the van, thinking, I'll be lucky if this is still here when we get back or maybe, it'll be four up on the car pyre.

I followed Renny through the industrial graveyard, then, just like Bermondsey, when we came to the river, it all opened up into a picture of freshness, opulence and grandeur. It was incredible. The divide was so deep, so noticeable. It was like crossing over a border into a different country.

Renny stopped at the beginning of Westminster Bridge to take the view in. Being a short bloke, it was impossible for him. There were so many people crossing, on their way to the march, he had to pull himself up onto the bridge railing to see.

Once he had secured himself, his head rotated left to Lambeth, then right to Westminster, taking it all in like I had, then his brow furrowed. "It's a different world Skinner, we're never going to live there, but we can get comfortable over there," he stated, pointing back to the wastelands.

I nodded and we filed in, joining the masses treading a path toward Parliament Square. To me it looked like a mass exodus from the wastelands. In some ways it was, but people had not just come from the wastelands of the South Bank to protest against the poor treatment of animals. They had come from far and wide, from all around the country to have their say, to tell the ruling classes that we didn't accept their exploitation of animals to feather their nests.

It was a great feeling, to be walking with so many like-minded people. It was empowering. It felt like we could change anything, everything. Today.

On entering Parliament Square, I felt the butterflies gnawing in my stomach. If Cerys has come, she'll be here, in this square, I thought. Letting Renny walk on, I halted, scanned the ALF stalls to see if I could see her. She wasn't there. She was never going to be here, I thought, it was a stupid dream of a stupid dreamer.

I shook it off, thinking, this isn't the right time for dreaming. It was a time for action, a time to protest, to show the rich they can't have it all their own way.

"Come on man, the march has already started, let's get moving," I told a confused Renny, who was now way out in front.

Mingling in with thousands of other latecomers, we raced up Parliament Street passing Downing Street.

The chorus went up.

"Maggie, Maggie, Maggie…"

"…Out, out, out!"

Renny and me joined in.

"Maggie, Maggie, Maggie…"

"…Out, out, out!"

"I'll tell you what Skinner, Robbo wants someone to knock out his movies for him, what do you reckon?" he shouted, over the chanting.

"What, 'Big Black Delivery' and 'Mothers Wishes'? Er, I don't know mate, not really my sort of thing," I said, as we weaved our way around a group of goths.

"You don't have to watch them; you just have to sell them."

"Seriously, I don't know anyone who'd want to buy them, well maybe a few," I answered, thinking of Ski Sunday, Coops and Mal.

"Well, there you go then, sorted."

"Nah, I don't think so… I don't mind knocking out a few pirates, but some of that stuff is bad news. Hillsey had something on with dogs in it, I mean come on man, I know he likes dogs but that is fucking sick."

Renny cracked up. "Oh yeah, Animal Farm - that's new in," he bellowed, just as the chanting lulled.

A couple of people looked around. "Oh, yeah, George Orwell, poignant stuff," I said, trying to look innocent.

Renny grinned, scanned our onlookers, and shouted, "No, it's the Private Films one, where all the animals fuck and get fucked."

I shook my head, grinned and picked up my pace, thinking, oh well, at least he's not still eating that pork pie.

Renny soon caught me up, and we picked up the pace some more.

On through Trafalgar Square, along The Mall, passing Buckingham Palace.

Eventually, we caught up with the main part of the march at Piccadilly. It was totally packed out, so we began to push, dodge and weave our way towards the front.

Boots, the chemists, came up on the left-hand side.

The chorus went up.

"Boots scum here we come!"

"Boots scum here we come!"

"Boots scum here we come!"

Inside the department store-sized shop, I could see the scared look on the staff's faces, as they drew back away from the large window at the front.

Suddenly, the window disintegrated, fell away.

A roar of appreciation rose up from the marchers.

"Boots scum here we come!"

"Boots scum here we come!"

"Boots scum here we come!"

In front of us, the march stalled, then there was a surge from behind as the people at the back pressed forwards, making the pressure build up.

I felt like I was being crushed. My chest heaved for oxygen to no avail.

I raised my head upwards, taking deep breaths in a vain attempt to get some air into my lungs. It was no good. It was like I was drowning in a sea of people.

Ramming my shoulder into the back of the person in front of me, trying to find some kind of relief, I saw Renny being dragged down in an undertow of arms and legs. I made a grab for his collar, got hold of it and heaved him up, but a crusty with white dreads came crashing down onto my arm.

Scything pain ripped up through me.

I let go and he was gone.

"Boots scum here we come!"

"Boots scum here we come!"

"Boots scum here we come!"

The crusty bobbed up, regaining his balance and cried out, "It's the fucking police, they've blocked off the road, they're pushing everyone back."

Craning my neck, I gaped over the mass of heaving bodies and saw the police steadily moving forward behind glinting Perspex shields.

All manner of objects were raining down on them. Pieces of blocks, parts of a keep left sign, sticks, bricks, even an old bike wheel spun at them.

I couldn't help laughing. The fucking wankers were really getting it. Reaching down, to see if I could find something to chuck, I got thrown backwards as another tide of bodies shoved forward. I thought I've had enough of this, I can't fucking breathe, I've got to get some space. I've got to get some space now. Locking my arms together on my chest, elbows jutting out, I spun around and around like a spinning top, ramming people until finally I could breathe.

"Oi, Skinnerrrrr."

My head spun again. I couldn't believe my eyes. There was Basher. Behind him, Chris Almond, a bent spliff hanging out of his grinning mouth.

I couldn't help smiling. "You alright lads? Thought you were in prison Bash?" I asked.

"What?" both said in unison.

I repeated, "Thought you were in prison Bash?", raising my voice.

Chris unplugged the spiff. "Nooo, he got out early for good behaviour didn't you Bash?"

Before Bash could answer he shouted, "Duck!" He covered his head, then cringed down.

Plastic water bottles bombarded us, pissing water all over us.

Chris came up, his spliff looked like a wet weekend in Skegness.

"Fucking hell," he bemoaned, dropping it.

Bash let out a snort. "I'm on parole at the moment If I get caught being a naughty boy again, I'll be back inside," he said, hoisting one of the bottles that had rained down on us in the direction of the advancing police.

Chris and me picked up a couple ourselves, joining in. None of them did any damage, though, they just bounced off the shields.

Other marchers were getting better shots off. Pieces of concrete were hurtling over our heads, but it didn't stop the advancing shield wall. The police just kept on coming. They were close now; I could see their faces, distorted behind the Perspex. Some were wide-eyed, clearly scared, others held their batons above their heads, resolute, vicious, ready to hurt.

Suddenly, on the left of me, there was a rush of people. There were police all around us. Basher kicked out with his steel toe caps and one of them screamed in agony and went down clutching his knee. Chris moved in, kicking the floundering copper until his compatriots hauled him up and dragged him away.

Pain ripped through my shoulder. Turning, I saw a determined-looking copper behind his shield. He raised his baton up to hit me again, and I charged into his shield. Immediately it fell inwards, and I went hurtling to the ground. From all sides hands grabbed me, bending my arms back. There was a sharp pinch as handcuffs snapped onto my wrists, then a knee came down hard on the small of my back.

"Aaaaahhh, you fuckers get off," I bellowed.

The knee dug in more.

I tried to turn over, to shake them off. "Aaaarrrrrggh, get off… You bastards… you're going to break my fucking back."

"If you keep struggling son, you're going to get hurt," a voice hissed into my ear.

I rolled left then right, turning, spinning, fighting with everything I had then eventually, just like the fly in the van, I tired, had nothing left and went limp.

"Are you done now? Good. Now we're going to lift you up and believe you me, if you struggle son, we'll put you right down again. It's up to you?" the voice hissed again.

I was spun over onto my front, then the four of them hauled me up, dragged me away down a side street and chucked me into the back of a waiting meat wagon.

A few moments later, there was an ear-shattering crash as something big hit the van's roof. Ducking down low, I cringed, waiting for more, then the back doors flew open, and a young-looking copper jumped in.

"Simon, for god's sake, drive!" he cried out.

"We've only got one, we need a couple more… Bloody newbie," replied one of the two cops in front.

Bricks hit the reinforced glass on the back door, and it split like a spider's web.

"For god's sake," screamed the newbie.

"OK, keep your hair on, you can explain to the duty sergeant why this little shit got his own chauffeur-driven van," said Simon, starting the motor.

Sirens blaring, lights flashing, we put distance between us and the riot.

I don't know why, but I actually felt like I was on top of the world; had conquered the world. I thought the adrenaline inside me must be turning my blood white.

Taking in my new surroundings, I started acclimatising myself. The copper sitting next to me had his head in his hands. He slowly shook his head from side to side.

Simon slammed the brakes on, and the newbie slid along the bench seat into me. "Sorry, mate," he apologised.

"Come on love, get out the bloody way. It's a siren dear. Yeah, that's it well done," came from the front, then, "If only her brain was the size of her tits… Oh, you stupid cow, get out of my fucking way."

The newbie turned to me, "I can't believe they're in the police force." I nodded my head, thinking, what is this? The legendary good cop, bad cop? This little wanker could have been the one who almost broke my fucking back a moment ago and now he wants to play best friends with me. He can fuck off.

"I joined the force to protect people. Not abuse them," he continued, scratching his long chin, thoughtfully, "I did three years at Hendon so I could join a bunch of misogynist bully boys."

Even though he was beginning to sound genuine, talking to him just didn't seem right. I'd spent most of my teenage years fearing and hating the police in equal measures. Now this one was opening up to me. Fuck knows why. If he was doing the good cop thing, it didn't make any sense. I was caught, done in and whatever was coming was going to come, no matter how this one was behaving.

"My dad was in the police, so was his dad," he continued. "I wasn't sure I wanted to join... Family tradition, I suppose."

On and on he went, and by the time we jerkily pulled up outside of Marylebone police station I was beginning to think he was on the level.

The back doors opened, flooding us with light. I stood up squinting. As I got out of the van, the newbie pushed my head down, so I didn't bang it on the low door frame.

"Bloody hell," he stated, looking at a queue of coppers and handcuffed rioters who were waiting to go inside.

"It's alright Simon, I'll take it from here. You go back to the riot and enjoy yourself," he winked at his compatriot.

Simon laughed. "OK, he's your collar, bloody newbies," he called out.

The newbie slammed the doors shut. "It's like the bloody January sales, isn't it?"

I was determined not to say anything, but when a couple of despatch riders hammered past, the newbie saw the wonder on my face.

"Oh, do you like bikes?"

"Yeah." I concurred.

"I've got a Honda CB 750, beautiful bike it is," he told me. "What have you got?"

"I haven't got one yet. I'm thinking of doing my test, so I can be a despatch rider... I'm not sure though, I live out in the sticks."

"If you want to do it, you should do it, don't let anyone tell you what to do with your life, you've only got one."

Oh what, I thought, this is surreal, I've just been nicked, and this copper is telling me to live my life the way I want to. That's exactly what I have been doing, and now I'm here. Talk about irony, fucking hell.

In the end, I just nodded dumbly, and we carried on waiting in silence to be booked in by the duty sergeant. It took a while, a long while. Time seemed to have slowed down since we'd got to the police station, but finally we got there.

The newbie stepped forward. "Arrested for threatening behaviour, affray, and assaulting a police officer."

"Bollocks, I was the one that was assaulted."

"OK, OK, stay calm. You'll have a chance to have your say in a minute, do you understand the charges?"

"Yeah." I conceded.

"Thank you, PC, good work, if you can remove his handcuffs, we'll take it from here." the desk sergeant said.

I watched the little bastard with his hands on me. You fucking snake, I thought, you almost had me there. No, you did have me there. I was too easy. It's no wonder that people don't think I'm ready.

Once I was booked in, I was taken to a holding cell. Pausing at the door, the copper told me that because they were so busy with the riot, I'd be sharing.

I wandered in and the door slammed behind me.

On the cot in the corner, lay an old bloke of about fifty. As I came in, his eyes pinged open and he sat up.

"You alright?" he greeted me in a friendly tone.

"Yeah," I said, distractedly, pulling a readymade out of my baccy pouch.

"Give me one then," he grinned.

"No," I told him.

"You'll get done in prison with an attitude like that."

I shrugged my shoulders, thinking, who does this grandad think he is?

"By the time you leave this cell you'll be offering me your baccy" he predicted and lay back down on the cot.

Oh shut up you old git, I thought. Who are you? Jimmy fucking Boyle?

Ignoring him, I lit up, took a big pull, blew it in his direction, sat back, and felt the calming effect of nicotine pulsing around my system.

I felt good for a moment, but the soporific effect soon eased out my rampaging adrenaline and the reality of my situation became clear.

I had been arrested for what sounded like a serious offence, a serious offence that could have me locked away, not just for months, but years.

Basher and his mates seemed to think of it as an occupational hazard. It wasn't for me though, I thought I was cleverer than them. I didn't think I was going to get caught, but I had, and it could mean me taking my turn behind the door. I didn't think I could do prison, be locked up 24 hours a day. I would go fucking insane.

I started feeling vulnerable, lost, and lonely.

Nobody I knew was even aware I was here, which was probably a good thing really. It wouldn't last though, during my booking in, the duty sergeant had asked me for proof of my ID and when I had produced my wallet, all I'd had was a tenner and a piece of paper with Cerys's name and phone number scrawled on it.

Fuck knows where my driver's license had got to. I hadn't seen it since the day before I'd been out with Del and Joyce.

I had no ID and was told that without any kind of verification of who I was, I could be locked up overnight. It was time to make a difficult decision, one that could cause me even more problems, but sitting in a cell with this old twat wasn't an option. It was time to let someone know, it was the only way out.

No way I was going to let them get in contact with my mum and dad, I'd given them enough grief over the years. It was either Cerys or Pete and Badwitch.

In the end, it had to be Pete and Badwitch. It would be bad enough the police to go around to see them, especially with how things were, but laying my troubles at Cerys's doorstep would be far worse. It would be well out of order. Even though she'd chucked me in the worst possible way, I couldn't do that to her.

I'm not sure how long I sat in silence, going over the various scenarios in my mind, but I was in a bad way by the time the light had gone from the tiny window above the cot.

"How old are you? About twenty?" came from the bloke on the cot.

"Nineteen," I replied.

"First time in?" he enquired, sitting up.

"Yeah," I told him, dropping my head.

He stretched his arms out, crucifix-like. "I remember my first time in, shits you up, don't it?"

I nodded minutely.

"I was only fifteen. I used to run around with a bunch of older lads, they'd never tell me much about what they were up to, I didn't care, I just liked the adventure."

I inhaled deeply, looked up and he put his hand out. "My name's Arthur." he grinned.

"Mick, well, Skinner."

"Give us one of those roll-ups, I'm gasping here, Mick, well, Skinner," he smiled broadly.

I snorted. "There you go mate," I laughed, handing him over the pouch.

Arthur and me sat back, smoking my baccy, and chatting for hours, then finally the cell door swung open, and I was told I was being released.

I couldn't believe it, I thought, I'm free, I've got away with it, but when I picked up my meagre possessions at the desk, I was told I would need to attend Hertford police station the following week. It wasn't the best news, but from what Arthur had told me, it wasn't the worst news either. It meant that they didn't have enough evidence to charge me then and there and they were still making their inquiries.

Once I'd got my stuff, I was escorted to the door. It opened and I was back on the street again.

I started walking, then strutting, kicking up my heels. A smile grew on my face, which soon turned into a laugh.

Fucking police, I thought, what a bunch of wankers. They've got nothing on me. I'm a free man. I felt like jumping, throwing my hands in the air, shouting it out like number six on the TV show, The Prisoner. Then I stopped laughing, stopped walking. I knew where the van was, but I didn't how to get there.

A few thoughtful moments later I strolled into a newsagent and came out with an A to Z inside my leather, thinking, I'm learning. I've got this sussed.

Opening the small book, I traced a line with my finger between where I was and Leake Street, where the van was parked up. It went directly through the centre of where the riot had been. There was no way I was getting through there.

So, I bunked the tube at Marble Arch and after a few changes I wandered out of Waterloo station back into the wasteland of the South Bank.

In the darkness, it looked even worse, a scarred, ravaged ghost land, the empty warehouses, the tombstones of British industry.

Now and again, I ducked into the shadows, as groups of lads came into view. I knew I was vulnerable on my own out here.

Soon I found the van, and with a great feeling of relief, achievement. I jumped in, started it up and opened the A to Z again.

Once I had plotted a course to the A1M, I depressed the clutch, put it in gear, then thought about the money stashed under the shotgun seat.

Looking around stealthily, I took it out of gear, flipped the locks down on the doors, flicked the interior light on, and reached under the seat. There it was. It felt solid in my hands. There must be thousands of pounds here, I thought.

I had to look; I couldn't help myself. Keeping the envelope low in the footwell I peeked inside. They were all 50s. I was wrong, there were tens of thousands.

Bang bang, BANG.

There was knocking on the window above me.

I looked up and there was a tramp with a polystyrene cup in his hand. "You got any spare change mate?"

"No, I fucking haven't," I replied, shoving the cash back under the seat.

Speeding off, leaving him behind, I thought, how the fuck did he end up like that? Did he fuck his life up? Or did life fuck him up? That I would never know, but I knew one thing, nothing and no one was going to fuck me up. I had done well knocking out weed to my mates, very well - I was going to do even better with the swords - but I knew my luck would run out one day.

Today, I had seen two different futures. One was the police cells with an old man reminiscing about a life going in and out of prison. The other is the excitement of being paid to ride motorbikes for a living.

It was an easy choice; I was going to ride my way to a decent living and have a fucking good laugh while I did it. I could do it too. With the money I'd made over the last few months, I would do my bike license. Then I would buy myself a decent road rocket. Get up here and do it.

The journey up to London from the Farm had only taken an hour and a half. With all the diversions around London because of the riot, it took double that on the way back. It was one o'clock in the morning when I drove up its familiar streets. Instead of going home, I stopped outside of Renny's place and knocked the door.

A light came on in the hall, then the door opened.

I stitched a smile onto my face. "Hi Mrs Reynolds, sorry it's so late, is Dean about?"

"Hi Mick, oh, don't worry about me, I'm watching an old Humphrey Bogart film, I don't sleep well these days," she said, fussing with her dressing gown.

"Skinner, where the fuck have you been?" came from behind her.

Mrs Reynolds moved aside testily, "Oh Renny, do mind your language."

Renny grinned. "Sorry nan," he told her quite sincerely, then he slipped past her and we walked over to the van.

"Renny, fucking hell, what a day that was…"

"Where's that fucking money Skinner?" he demanded, cutting across me.

No that was it, I'd had enough now, I squared up to him. "Who the fuck, you think you're talking to, you short-arse little cunt?"

He didn't say anything. Just steadily watched me.

"I'm fed up with this bullshit, I'm not a fucking idiot," I spat.

"Alright calm down, where's the money?"

"In the van, under the seat, where you fucking left it."

Renny leant into the van, snatching up the envelope while I dropped into the driver's seat and turned the engine over.

"Skinner, cheers for this, I owe you one."

"Yeah, you fucking do mate."

"Don't tell Robbo what happened," he told me and slammed the door.

I snorted, put my foot on the accelerator and raced back to Longwood Road.

Hoisting myself out of the van, I stretched out my aching back, making it pop a couple of times. I sighed, looking around.

Sometimes, it was hard to believe there were so many people living around here, it was so quiet, I thought.

Sighing again, I started the short walk over to my block. A bite to eat and a nice little spliff before a decent night's sleep was the plan, but as I walked into the hallway, I noticed the TV was on in the sitting room. Not only was it unusual, the TV being on this late, it was unusual that someone was actually in the sitting room at all, especially Pete and Badwitch. Most of the time, they'd run upstairs when they heard me coming in. It didn't bode well, but whatever was going on, after the day I'd had, I was ready for anything.

I pounded in. Pete looked up from the bright tube.

"Skinner, we've had the police around about you."

I pulled a smile. "I got nicked at an antivivisection march in London."

"Oh my god, you were there? The Smiths were up there too. We were planning on going, but Janine's grandmother's been, well you know, she's been ill," he said, shifting in his chair.

"Yeah, I thought it was your kind of thing, thought you might be there."

He shook his head sadly. "No… Unfortunately not."

"Where is Janine?"

"Oh, she's at her mum's, trying to keep her spirits up."

"Is she? Oh no," I commiserated with him. "I've got an idea," I said, turning.

I raced upstairs, grabbed an eighth of personal out of my ounce of personal, wrapped it in a bit of cling film and took it down to him.

My thinking was that if it's a love/hate thing with dealers, then getting the love from your snooty landlord's boyfriend is a wise move. I still charged him an extra landlord's fee though. I wasn't a total sycophant.

Pete and me sat back watching the Animals live on the BBC while having our first smoke together. It was good to be home, good to feel comfortable again. I let the smoke and the music wash over me. Soon enough, I was relaxing deep into my seat, nodding along to the sixties-style beats. I only knew one of their tracks, 'The House of the Rising Sun.' I recognised its haunting guitar intro straight away.

"This is a great track man," I said dozily.

"It's the best," said Pete, reaching over to me.

As Pete handed me the spliff, the phone rang.

I baulked on the spliff, jumped up, legged into the kitchen, and grabbed the receiver.

"Hello?"

Silence.

"Hello?" I demanded.

I heard panting like a dog.

"Now then, now then, now then, guys and girls, guys and girls," I Jimmy Saville-ed. "Jimmy Saville? Come in Jimmy, can you hear me? I laughed. "Savy? Are you there? …Cunt." I taunted.

"You wanker. How's Hertford these days, Skinner?" a voice suddenly came through.

I snorted. "Lovely at this time of the year, when you coming down, dear?"

Click.

The line went dead.

Chapter Twelve

Paranoid John Loses Control

One minute I was asleep, the next, I was bouncing down the stairs to stop the incessant ringing of the phone. If it was that wanker Savy again, I was going to rip the wire out of the fucking wall.

Grimacing, I picked up the phone ready to let fly, but it was Hugh.

Hugh was very animated this morning. Between great gulps of breath, he told me that we wouldn't be working in the annexe today, because after years of negotiations, Herts Archaeological Unit had finally got the go-ahead from Lord Laing, of Laing construction fame, to dig in his colossal cellar at Hunsdon House.

There'd been rumours going around about this for a while, but nobody thought it would actually happen. Even I got excited.

Hugh had told us all about it when we were working in the annexe.

Hunsdon House had been built and rebuilt many times since its first incarnation around the middle of the 15th century, so on the surface there wasn't much of interest, but digging in the huge cellar underneath would be like going back in time. Hugh reckoned we would find loads of valuable artefacts from what he called 'King Henry VIII's hunting lodge.'

Logistically, it was going to be a nightmare, though.

All the soil dug up in the cellar would have to be barrowed up a series of steep winding steps on wooden planks. Then, once we managed to get the barrow outside, it would have to be pushed up another steep slope and loaded into a trailer. The trailer would then be attached to a tractor and driven off to a slag heap which sat next to an ancient wooden barn on the other side of the house.

It sounded dangerous. It sounded like a lot of hard work, but it also sounded like a lot of fun, so I was well up for it. My driving duties were to be upped too.

In the morning, I would have to pick up the Hertford lot, take them to the dig in Ware, then wait while Hugh sorted out who was staying in Ware and who would go on to Hunsdon. I had been expecting something like this from the moment they handed me the keys to the van, so it wasn't a problem. I'd just have to get up earlier and be on time for my pick-ups. I thought it was still a small price to pay.

Hugh told me he'd see me in Ware in an hour or so, which gave me plenty of time to splash some water on my face and get a bit of breakfast.

Once I had eaten, I checked the sitting room. Pete was crashed out in his chair; I guessed Badwitch must still be at her mums' place. I didn't like seeing Pete like that, without his girlfriend around he had completely lost it. Not that I felt guilty, if he wanted to stay up all night watching TV puffing weed that was up to him, even if I had sold it to him. He was nineteen, old enough to make his own choices.

"Oi Pete, wake up, the house is on fire," I laughed.

Pete pulled a smile, his head lolling forward. "Put it out on your way out, mate."

I cackled back, left him to Breakfast Time and got myself moving.

Being up early on the Farm wasn't so bad these days. I knew all my neighbours, knew what they did for a living. The majority of people here were just doing what they needed to do, to feed themselves and their families - keep things ticking over.

As I drove up Tudor Way, I saw a familiar sight. Hillsey was being hauled along toward the shop by the zoo. I wound my window down and pulled over. "Oi, Hillsey! I shouted hitting the horn.

He almost jumped out of his skin, then seeing it was me, he pinched a smile.

"How you going man?" I asked.

"Yeah, good Skinner, I'm on a nice little earner. I'm knocking out videos for Robbo. I've got all sorts. You interested? He enquired, scratching at his ear.

"Nah, I'll give it a miss mate," I parried the young businessman.

"You sure? I've got all the latest," he kept at it.

"Nah mate… How's the zoo these days?" I asked, changing the subject, glancing at the dogs. "Oh what, where's Stinky Terrier?" I asked, searching the pack for the plucky little terrier.

Hillsey slumped forward. "He's gone."

"Oh, what? Nooo!" I exclaimed, horrified.

"Yeah, he ate Renny's cannabis plant, so I called up Carol, you know Bash's sister? And Bash showed up and took him home before Renny came back."

"Oh, nice one, so he's back with Bash, is he?"

"No, Bash got nicked at some riot in London and he's back inside. Carol's looking after him now. I'm really missing little Stink... We all are, aren't we?" he said, gazing lovingly at his seven little friends.

"Oh well, as long as he's OK. Right, mate, I'd better get on." I told him, sticking the van in gear.

"You sure you don't want any videos? I'm doing 'The Muppets Take Manhattan,' 'The Ewok Adventure' and 'Big Black Delivery' for a tenner, special."

I put my hand up. "Nah, seriously it's fine," I called over my shoulder.

The next stop was Tanks' place on Raynham Street. He was expecting me, so I tooted the horn and sat back, waiting for the big rocker to show.

On the porch of his house, I saw something bike shaped under some red tarpaulin. I piled out, legged it up his garden path, heaved the tarp off to reveal an old FS1E. Creasing up laughing, I wandered back to the van and made myself comfortable.

A few moments later his front door sprung open, and he shouldered out, giving me a big grin. That big grin soon faltered though, when he noticed his FS1E was in full view. Puzzled, he looked at it for a while then over at me.

Throwing my arm out my window I twisted my hand backwards and forward. "Weee weee, wee, I like your Fizzy tank."

Tank cracked up laughing, hastily covered up the little yellow Yam, then he mockingly trudged over sheepishly, taking shotgun.

Tank pulled out his roll-ups, beginning to make us a couple of smokes. "I'm the only biker in the world who doesn't have a bike," he explained.

"Don't worry about it, I'm getting a ped too mate, I want to be a despatch rider - going to do it up in London."

Tank licked the paper, then shook his head. "Don't do it Skinner, when you stop despatching, you'll never ride again."

I snorted, thinking, of course I will, why wouldn't I? With the money I'll be making as a circuit rider, I'd be able to buy a really decent one if I did stop.

"Says the only biker in the world who doesn't have a bike."

"Seriously the winters will kill you."

I sighed, still not believing it, stuck it in gear, put my foot on the accelerator. Then raised it up again. Coming out of the house opposite, I saw Cerys's mate, Jackie, in a nurse's uniform. She saw me, waved, and came over beaming,

"Whatcha Tank? You alright Skinner?"

"Hi Jackie, like the uniform, it really suits you."

"Cheers Skinner," she smiled, brushing the long blue and white garment flat. "One size fits nobody."

I cracked up. "You're doing OK then?"

"Really good, yes really enjoying it. After I've qualified, I'm hoping to work at Great Ormond Street."

"Oh, nice one, sounds good… So, how's Cerys?" I blundered in.

Her smile faded. "She's fine yeah, still working hard."

"Did she tell you?"

"Yeah, shame really, you two were good together."

Tank started humming the violin passage from the film 'Love Story.'

Jackie grinned. "Oh, shut up Tank."

"Yeah, shut up Tank." I backed her up.

It was useless, I couldn't have this kind of conversation with Tank about, it would just give him ammunition for later, so I put my foot back on the accelerator.,

"The next time you see her can you put in a word for me?" I asked.

"Yeah, I'll put a word in for you, Skinner."

"Thank you, Jackie."

She nodded, pointing at the van. "That's a funky van you've got there, looks like the Pope mobile."

I chuckled. "Yeah, this is Pope Tank the FS1E here," I told her throwing my thumb in Tank's direction.

She creased up. "Weeee, weeee," she mimicked twisting her wrist.

"Cheers Jackie, see you," I said laughing, as we pulled away.

I put my foot down. "Right, it's Paranoid John next."

"Fuck, turn around, I need my ear plugs." laughed Tank.

I threw the wheel left at the junction, then we sped off along Ware Road.

"I was going to ask you, why does he spend so much time bullshitting?" I questioned.

"He doesn't."

"What? So, he's really met all those people, has he?" I returned sceptically.

"No, not all of them, but he thinks he has."

"I don't get it, why is he called Paranoid John then? Surely, he should be called Delusional John?"

"Don't know." he shook his head, flicking ash out of the window. "Doesn't have the same ring to it, does it? He's the one that made it up."

"What's his real name then?"

Tank cracked up laughing. "If I told you, you wouldn't believe me."

"Go on then."

"No, you won't believe me."

"Come on Tank."

"Kenneth Kendall."

"Fuck off Tank."

"I told you."

***

Once I had picked up Paranoid John, Hippy John, Viv, Astrid, and Kath'll, I drove us to Ware to find out who was going where. It turned out to be a complete waste of time because when we got there, Hugh told me that the Ware site was still waterlogged, so we were all going over to Hunsdon.

I had driven through Hunsdon a few times. It was on the scenic route between my old village and Harlow. It looked quite a lot like my old village too, nestled in its quiet countryside setting. The one main difference between the two villages was that Hunsdon didn't have four pubs. Thundridge was the only village I knew that had four pubs.

I could have taken the faster route on the A414, but I was in no hurry, so I took the slower scenic route through the villages. In the back, Tank and Paranoid John shifted uncomfortably as I steered us around the meandering turns into Wareside.

"Does anyone know anything about bikes? You see there's a bloke selling one here," I asked, taking my eyes off the road.

Everyone fell about laughing.

Tank grinned. "How does bollocks sound?"

"That won't do nicely," I quipped.

Paranoid John looked up brightly. "I used to do freakouts... I once freaked out Bowie with a cigar and a magnet. It was in the summer of 69, a week before I had smoked grass with Princess Margaret, two months before I did backing vocals on Marc Bolan's Jeepster, a week before I found a herring in my back pocket after I dropped acid at Jaggers' flat, a year after..."

I grabbed Voivod's 'War and Pain,' slammed into the cassette player, twisted the volume up to maximum and drowned out the droning.

Hunsdon House soon loomed large on the horizon. It was easy to see, but not so easy to find the entrance, as the estate it was on was absolutely massive. Finally, after driving around for half an hour Tank spotted a small sign deep in a privet hedge with 'Hunsdon Whores' written on it. I cracked a smile, thinking, the kids in the village were just like we used to be. Bloody little hooligans.

Spinning the steering wheel, I took us off the narrow B road onto a gravel track. Straight away, the ungainly Fiat began to bounce from side to side.

Tank, gave me a sly look, creased up laughing. I knew what I had to do.

I floored it, then began throwing the steering wheel violently from left to right. There was absolute pandemonium in the back, people were getting chucked around like rag dolls, me and Tank were in tears.

I kept it going for a while longer, but as we thundered out of a small copse the track became a long sweeping driveway in full view of the house.

Hugh had told everybody that we had to be on our best behaviour, so I took my foot off the metal, checked the mirror, assessing the damage in the back.

Viv was on top of Astrid, while both Hippy John and Paranoid John were on top of Kath'll. Everyone looked satisfied. I could see Paranoid John's lips moving. He was going on about something or other. I didn't know, as thankfully, 'War and Pain' was still blaring out from the console in front of us.

Tank tapped me on the leg, turning my attention to the vast Hunsdon House, with its ornate surrounding gardens.

Immaculately manicured grass led to lines of tightly clipped conifers which navigated their way around a series of fountains.

As we got closer to the house, remembering Hugh's words of warning once again, I turned the music down. Thankfully, Paranoid John had fallen silent, so all we could hear now was the van's wheels scrunching pleasantly on the gravel drive.

Hugh had told me to go to the back of the property and wait for him there, but when we had finally traversed the rambling house, he was already waiting, one hand on his hip, the other on the roof of his light blue Volvo estate.

"Skinner, nice of you to join us," he said sarcastically.

"Sorry Hugh, we couldn't find it."

"Yes, tiny isn't it," he mused. "Come on people, let's get this show on the road," he told us, beckoning with his hand.

Hugh assigned Hippy John and me to set up the planks to barrow up the loose from the cellar, while the rest of them disappeared down the flight of stairs into the darkness with forks and shovels to take off the top layer of soil.

It was a proper puzzle, or as Hugh had told us quite rightly, it was a logistical nightmare.

On the way up from the cellar there were two flights of stairs. The first one went from the cellar to a small holding area outside of the old kitchens. The second, up to ground level. Our main problem was that the planks we were given weren't long enough to reach the top of the staircases. It took us a while to work it out, but the only way it would work was to lay four planks on the stairs, tie them together, then balance another four planks at their ends, to cover the top part of the stairs.

Once that was done, we put a 'barrow plank' across the top and Hippy John went and got Hugh. He was happy with our work, but he reckoned we needed to nail the planks together to stop them from moving under the weight of the barrows. It made sense to us, so I fetched the hammer I had been keeping under my driver's seat since my journey back from the riot. Then me and Hippy John knocked the nails into place. It looked good. It was time for a test run.

Volunteering, I strutted down the stairs with Hugh and Hippy John following and found Tank trying to put another shovel load into an already full barrow.

Hugh cracked up. "Oh, come now, Tank take some of that out," he said.

"No, no, no, I'm fine," I proclaimed, flexing my arms for effect.

Viv giggled coltishly. "Zowwie caveman," she grinned, watching me pulling the barrow backwards, getting myself a run-up.

"Go on then, Skinner!" said Astrid.

Pat and Nick clapped their hands, counting down.

"Five... Four... Three... Two... one … GO!"

I took a deep breath, picked the barrow up and ran at the steep incline of stairs with everything I had. The first wheel hit the middle plank and I galloped up.

As I reached the join between the planks the wheelbarrow lurched forwards. The wheel flew out from the side of the barrow, then the whole lot fell backwards and crashed back down the steps into the cellar. I couldn't do anything but watch.

Hugh's head popped tentatively around the corner of the cellar. "Bloody hell, Skinner are you alright?"

I was totally stunned; I didn't know what to say.

Eventually, I said, "Yeah… I think so," as I slowly traipsed down the stairs. "The wheel, it just… it just… came off."

Down in the cellar, everyone crowded around the barrow, watching Hugh twiddle his moustache, like Poirot, trying to work out what happened.

I took another deep breath, looking over at Tank.

He was standing behind the others, with a big grin on his face, waving a small spanner in his hand.

Tank handed it to Hugh, who was so absorbed in the situation he totally missed the connection and began to put the barrow together again.

I fell about laughing.

Hugh glanced up, his face a picture of concern. "Are you sure you're alright Skinner? Maybe you should go and have a sit down for a few minutes."

I shook my head at both the wind-up merchant and the failed Poirot, picked up another full barrow and was off.

Bam, onto the first plank.

Bam, bam, where the planks joined.

Bam, into the recess.

I took a deep breath, then heaved the barrow up the top staircase and out into the daylight.

I heard muted cheering from the cellar, took one more deep breath and pushed the barrow up the slope to the waiting tractor and trailer.

"It was a piece of piss," I told Muncher as he waited at the side of the trailer, shovel in one hand, roll-up in the other.

"Was it," he said, but not like a question, more like he couldn't be arsed to say anything else.

Two words today, I thought, that beats yesterday's record by one. Then, Muncher really surprised me.

"This tractor does 15 miles an hour tops," he told me, digging into the loose.

"Yeah? It looks pretty old, doesn't it?" I replied, surprised by his cascade of words.

"It's a Ferguson TE20, from the 1950s. Not in bad condition either."

"Nice one Munch, you know your tractors mate."

Munch nodded back.

It looked like that was all I was going to get today, so I picked up the barrow and took it down for another load.

One hour of calf-burning barrow work later, I swapped over with Nick, while Tank swanned off to drive the tractor. You lucky git, I thought, I wanted to do that. It wasn't down to me though, it was Hugh's call, so I despondently picked up a shovel and stalked back down into the cellar.

Even before I'd got to the recess, I felt the chill of dampness in the air. By the time I'd got down in the cellar, the air was wet with condensation. It was almost pitch black too-way from the steps, the only light being thrown out was coming from a couple of portable camping lamps. This is absolutely fucking ridiculous, I thought, there's more light in a mummy's arsehole than down here, we'll find fuck all, we'll be lucky to find ourselves at the end of the day.

In the shadows of a huge mantle that ran along the west-facing wall of the cellar, the two girls worked swiftly with their shovels, heaving dark grey clay into Hippy John's barrow. I fell into line next to them, stuck my shovel in and got my head down. The going was good to start with, we moved a lot of soil; Hippy John, Nick and Paranoid John all had to barrow for us, but as we dug deeper into the clay the wetter it got. It became back-breaking work.

"Fuck this," announced Viv, "Get Hugh, this must be deep enough."

I nodded. Dropping my shovel, I started to walk up.

Back on the surface, Hugh was chucking the topsoil and clay from a spilt barrow load into the trailer, while Tank sat in the tractor driver's seat puffing away happily. I thought, you dossing bastard. It was no real surprise though; I'd seen it happen time and time again. People would be bursting their lungs and there'd be Tank kicking back, lost in a cloud of Golden Virginia. The funny thing was, Tank could be such a charming character that nobody would mind. Not me though.

"Oi Tank, Viv wants you down in the cellar."

Tank cracked up laughing.

Hugh glanced over his shoulder. "What is it, Skinner?"

"Viv reckons we're deep enough."

"How would she know?" cackled Tank, billowing out smoke.

"OK, come on then," said Hugh, chucking his shovel down. "And bring a trowel with you Skinner, you're going to do some proper archaeology today," he shouted over his shoulder.

"OK, nice one Hugh," I said, smiling smugly at Tank, walking to the van.

Tank grinned back and gave me the wankers sign, getting back to his roll-up.

I placed my hammer back under my seat, went around the back, grabbed a trowel, and followed Hugh underground.

Back in the cellar, the shovelling had stopped. Everyone was down on their knees, trowels in hand, scraping over the clay. Already, large pieces of light grey pottery were being unearthed.

Astrid held a piece up in the dim light. "Look I've found Henry VIII's Demi Jar."

"Me too," said Pat, grinning. "Come on Skinner you need to catch up."

I bent down, scratching away at the surface and soon had a piece of Demi Jar myself. It was filthy, so I carefully peeled away the clay from its shell-like surface with my trowel. I nodded my head, smiling broadly. It was the top part with a small face moulded onto its handle. Turning it over so I could get the packed clay out of its inside, something glinted at me from the clay. I stopped, then very carefully, picked out the clay, brought it up to get a better look.

A small metallic object dropped down into the darkness.

"Shit," I whispered, falling to my knees.

I traced my hands over the clay. Soon I found it again.

Gripping it tightly, I raised it up and saw it was a coin.

I spat on it, rubbed it, pulled out my lighter, flicked a flame, taking another look.

On one side, there was a coat of arms, on the other a crown with a rose above it.

Examining it closely, it looked like bronze but when squeezed, it gave a little.

Hugh had told us to watch out for this with metals; gold was a soft metal until it was mixed. It's gold, I thought, oh my fucking god it's gold. This could be worth thousands of pounds. I was just about to put it in my pocket when I stopped. It just didn't seem right. I had nicked all those swords from the annexe, but that was just like stealing from a shop. It meant nothing. To actually find something though, something, someone had dropped over 500 years ago was really special.

I stood up. "Oi, you lot, have a look at this," I said, holding my find aloft.

Hugh scrambled over, followed by the rest. He took a small torch from his top pocket and clicked the light on.

"Bloody hell it's a Tudor Crown," he announced. "Well done, Skinner. That's amazing," he said, twirling it in his hand.

From all around hands patted me on the back.

Hugh placed the crown into a drawstring pouch he had for special finds. "I think you deserve a reward for that Skinner, how does a cigarette break sound?"

I said, "Cheers," as I started for the steps, hearing the rest of the diggers playfully moaning.

Hugh creased up. "Come on, it's only ten minutes until lunch, if we follow Skinner's example, we'll have another ten coins by then."

"Yeahhhhh, get to work you lazy sods," I bawled back at the foot of the steps.

On the surface, Tank sat on the tractor waiting for the trailer to be filled up. Nick pushed his barrow up the plank and upended it, followed by Muncher, followed by Hippy John, then they all went back for another load.

"You're on the doss today, Tank, come on, give someone else a go."

"Sorry Skinner, you're not qualified."

"Bollocks, you haven't even got a driver's license."

"Hugh wanted me to do it today, don't worry you'll get your turn," he laughed.

"Yeah right, and tomorrow you'll say you've got a bad knee or something and you need to be on light duties."

"Skinner, I'm actually hurt by that suggestion," he whined, then rubbed his knee, grimacing. "You know what, my knee has been playing up recently."

"Yeah, I bet it has," I said, watching Nick powering up the slope towards us.

"Oi Tank, Skinner's found a gold coin," he announced, aiming the barrow's front wheel with the plank on the trailer. "It's pure gold," he shouted, on the run.

Tank, boggled, turned to me. "Is that true?"

"Yeah, while you're sitting on your arse up here, we're finding decent stuff."

Nick emptied the barrow, skipped down the plank,

"Come and see."

Tank jumped down from the tractor, then stopped, looked at me, grinned and snatched the keys. "I'll take these," he chortled.

"Oh what, come on Tank, just a little go," I beseeched him.

"Sorry you're not qualified, I'm the only one who's qualified," he told me, and sauntered off with Nick, both of them laughing their heads off.

Once they were out of sight, I thought, fuck this, hopped up onto the seat. I must admit, I'd never seen such a shambolic piece of machinery in all my life.

Munch certainly knew his tractors. It was old alright; in places it had been bodged too - but not in the way a mechanic would do it. More in the way a kid would do it.

Instead of an accelerator pedal, it had something that resembled a horse riding stirrup.

On the other side, the brake was the same, but I could actually see the brake wire attachment connected to the stirrup.

Before I knew what I was doing, I unhooked it, then I hooked up again, then after a quick glance around, I unhooked it again, thinking, there is a hand brake, and Tank is qualified.

I fast walked back to the top of the steps, began hopping down two at a time, and almost collided with the diggers hauling themselves up.

"Oi, gold finger," laughed Pat.

"Gold finger, gold finger," sang Tank, cracking up.

Hugh was the last one up the steps.

"I'll tell you what, that was a fabulous find. Finds like this will ensure the funding of the unit for years to come."

"Cheers, Hugh," I said, trying to follow the rest up.

"I believe it's only the start; there's so much more history for us to dig up... And believe you me, we'll find it."

I thought this is great, but not now.

"Yeah, I bet," I replied, dodging to one side to go around him.

"I'm going to call the Hertfordshire Mercury when I get home," he chimed, blocking my progress.

"That's great Hugh," I said, spinning back the other way.

"I think Herts Archaeological Unit... Could be front page news," he said, blocking me off again.

"Great news, incredible," I said, going to the left this time.

"Oh, yes of course… Come on now, let's get some lunch," he said, turning.

I fell into line behind him, got to the top of the slope and my jaw dropped open.

Paranoid John was sitting on the tractor.

"Oh no, no, no..." I stammered.

Paranoid John bowed deeply to Viv and gunned the engine twice, sending smoke billowing out of the upright exhaust pipe: he was off.

"What the bloody hell is he doing?" scowled Hugh.

"I don't know Hugh," I cried, rooted to the ground.

Paranoid John approached the edge of the car park, pressed down with his left foot on the brake. Nothing happened. He tried again. Still nothing happened. In a panic, he pressed down on the right pedal, the accelerator, and it speeded up, sending the tractor careering through an ornate hedge and out onto a croquet lawn.

"Oh, bloody hell," whispered Hugh, totally dumbstruck.

"Oh, bloody hell," I echoed.

Paranoid John spun the wheel, turning the tractor in a long arc, cutting deep lines into the clipped grass, then disappeared behind a hedge at the side of the car park. All we could hear was the thumping of the engine, then a few moments later, he reappeared, ripping through a hedge, and rolled into the back of Hugh's Volvo.

"Oh no," Hugh whimpered, "Not, my Volvo."

Tank fell about laughing.

"It's not bloody funny Tank," cried Hugh, already running.

Viv and Astrid were first to the tractor, followed by the rest of us.

Paranoid John wasn't hurt, he just sat there staring, his eyes almost popping out from under his curtain-like hair.

I let out a sigh of relief.

Viv patted him on the shoulder and carefully helped him down.

Arms out to his sides, he jerkily walked up to me and Tank, like a Thunderbirds puppet, then he stopped, furrowed his brow. "It's like Marc Bolan all over again. Yes, I was with him on that fateful day. It was the day after I fell off Big Ben, protesting about the war, the same week I went poaching with Mott the Hoople, the month I went tobogganing with Bowie."

Tank and me shared a glance.

"Oh well, he's alright then," said Tank.

I nodded. "Yep."

***

In the dying embers of the day, I lay back on my bed watching the rays of sunlight streaming through my open window, thinking back to the events. Finding that coin had been great, better still knowing that it would lead to more financing from the Manpower Services, but it got me thinking about the swords. OK, it felt like I was stealing from a shop at the time but maybe it wasn't so simple. Maybe, somebody had felt the same way I did when I found my coin, maybe, their find had led to more funding too. I didn't know but one thing I was certain of was that I couldn't turn back time and even though the idea of planting the swords in the cellar back at Hunsdon house was appealing, especially if Tank found them. I wasn't going to risk it. I wasn't going to leave the swords under my bed either so in the end, it was simple, I thought, fuck it, I want a road rocket and there's no time like the present.

On my way out, I heard the TV blaring out the news, so I thought I'd say hi to Pete but when I knocked open the door, the sitting room was empty.

Snorting, I wandered in, turned the flood of lies off, opened the window to let out the stink of weed from our session last night, then headed for the door.

Walking out through the yards, I wriggled the two swords I had wedged down the back of my leather into a more comfortable position.

I walked up Longwood Road, turned left onto the Ridgeway and spotted Jason Brown shouldering his way up the road towards me. I smirked at the bloated wanker. His head dropped and his shoulders narrowed. Good job too, I've got more than a rolling pin on me, I thought, feeling the cold steel on my skin.

Lenny the Lamp's place looked as raked out as ever. The council still hadn't fixed the door the police had knocked in when they raided the party.

I pounded my fist on it, waiting.

Brandon answered. "You alright Skinner? Come in mate," he said brightly, "You seen Renny about much?"

I shook my head. "Nah, I've been staying in most nights, puffing. I've been knackered after work."

"Oh right, he's been wondering where you've been," he said, grimacing. "You should go and see him," he laughed.

"I'm going up to his after here."

"I would if I was you."

"Oh yeah. Why?"

"No, no, I'm not going spoil the surprise," Brandon chuckled. "So…" he said, getting to it, opening his hands.

"Is Robbo about?" I asked.

"No, mate, he's house hunting in the countryside, he won't be back for ages … Alright for some, eh? I'm managing the shop tonight."

"I've got more of those swords, I got two this time," I stated.

"Have you? Nice one, we like them."

"Here you go," I said, pulling them out.

Brandon felt the weight of it, then twisted it around. "Oh yes, yes, very nice, how much did Robbo say?"

"They're two hundred each mate."

Brandon chuckled to himself. "He said that did he?" he exclaimed, a big grin cutting his pockmarked face. "OK right you are sir, four hundred it is. Wait there."

I sighed, thinking about Brandon's response.

Now I knew for sure why Renny had said that we were both going to do well out of the swords. He was taking a cut. It didn't surprise me though; I'd have done the same thing myself. The thought that Brandon may be doing it too pissed me off, but where else was I going?

Nowhere. Lenny the Lamp's place had the monopoly on dodgy goods; if I wanted to pass GO and collect my two hundred quid, there was always going to be a fee to pay.

Brandon returned. Still grinning, he handed me eight fifties. I thanked him and left, thinking, I'm getting a bit of that money I brought back from London after all.

Back on the Ridgeway I strutted along feeling like I was a made man.

BMWs weren't usually seen on the Farm, so when I saw one cruising down the road towards me, I began to wish I still had those swords.

If it's those posh Cambridge wankers, I thought, they'll never catch me, I know the blocks and yards like the back of my hand.

As it got closer, I still couldn't make out who it was as the windows were blacked out.

Then it stopped.

One of the windows slid down revealing Renny's smiling face. Behind, leaning around him, a peroxide rocker girl stared. For a moment I thought it was Mia.

"Skinner, how you going? Long time no see."

"You alright? I was just coming up yours."

Renny nodded. "Brandon said. Do you like the motor?"

"Yeah decent," I returned, giving it a cursory once over. "I need to talk to you about something."

"Talk away, Carrie's alright." He turned his head towards her. "This is Skinner, by the way."

"Hello, Skinner."

I gave her a nod. "OK… I want my money for the sword, mate."

Renny smiled, pulled out a wad of fifties, counted out five and handed them over. "There's an extra fifty there for the driving."

"Cheers Renny, nice one, appreciate it," I told him, ramming them into my wallet with the others. "Just out of interest, what happened to you that day?"

Renny stuffed his wad back into his pocket.

"I got nicked by a snatch squad, got taken to Paddington nick. When I got out, I went back to Lambeth and the van was gone. I got the train home. Truth is, I thought you'd done the dirty on us."

I snorted. "Where would I go?"

"Well exactly… Look, we're going to see the Crumbsuckers and the Butthole Surfers. We'd better go," he told me, nodding at Carrie who smiled back.

"Cool, nice one. Have a good time, both of you."

"See, told you he was polite, didn't I?" Renny smirked.

Carrie beamed. "Thanks, Skinner."

Renny gunned the BMW's engine. "You made up your mind above that Savage Circle gig yet?"

"Nah not yet, I'll let you know," I said.

"Well don't wait too long, it's selling out fast."

Carrie, Renny and me said our goodbyes and I walked back towards home, watching the Farms' latest entrepreneur hurtle off down the Ridgeway.

A few minutes earlier I thought I was a made man, but now with six hundred and fifty quid in my wallet, I thought I was a capo.

Never before in my life had I seen this kind of money, and the cynic in me said that I would probably never see it again.

It was almost two months' pay.

Not only that, but I had another nine swords to sell and all the money from selling weed too. It was time to get a bike I could learn to ride on.

Taking my time, I strolled back through the yards, thinking about what bike I should get first when I noticed the kitchen light was on.

It looked like Pete was back. Good, I thought, we'll have a couple of spliffs, then I'm going to hit the hay, it's been a long day.

Before I even had the chance to get my key into the lock, Pete opened the door. He was instantly in my face.

"Skinner some blokes came around here looking for you," he babbled, furtively glancing right and left, "They said, when they caught up with you, you're dead."

"What else did they say?"

"Nothing, really, just to tell Skinner he's dead when we catch up with him."

"They're the wankers who've been calling us, mate."

Pete nodded thoughtfully. "Ah, I see, that makes sense."

"Oh well, fuck them," I declared. "I've got a couple of things that need doing, I'll be down later for a smoke yeah?" I bounded up the stairs.

In my bedroom, I decided that having a spliff at this moment in time probably wasn't the best idea. I needed to think about what my next move would be. I kicked my DMs off and lay on my bed. It didn't take me long.

I was going to go to their gig and fuck it up.

Chapter Thirteen

Savage Circle

Savage Circle's first single, 'Over Idiot Educated' was riding high in the indie charts, while some of the venues on their tour were already sold out. I couldn't believe for the life of me why they were still after me for nicking a few cannabis plants, we'd left most of them anyway. It made no sense.

In contrast, if it had been me, I'd have written them off as collateral damage and moved on, but they hadn't. They kept coming back and although they hadn't come around mine calling again, they'd been seen up on the Farm, cruising the Ridgeway in their Cabstar.

Ironically, both times, I'd only been about fifty feet away from the pricks, sitting in Lenny the Lamp's, puffing with Brandon, Renny and Shads.

If we'd known they were on our patch, it would have been the end of their silly little feud. We'd have fucking destroyed them.

It wasn't to be though, so I kept with my plan.

On the evening of Savage Circle's first gig of their tour 'Jesus Saves at the Nat West' at the Junction in Cambridge, I made my way up to Renny's, hoping he hadn't stayed over at Carrie's again. He had, so it was straight onto plan B. I made my way to Hertford North Station to catch the train.

As I walked down Welwyn Road past Fordham Rise, I started having doubts about my plans. Turning up on my own wasn't the best idea, even if they were 'posh wankers' as Renny called them. They were four posh wankers. I wasn't turning back now though; I'd just have to play it as I saw it at the time.

Inside my leather jacket, I heard the reassuring clink of the half bottle of rum I had hidden. I gave it a pat, thinking, I might need a bit of Dutch courage - well, in this case, Jamaican courage might be better - tonight.

There was nobody at the ticket office at the station, so I wandered on through the gate, piled on the first train, broke the seal on the rum and got stuck in.

Savouring the rich caramel taste, I grabbed a discarded Hertfordshire Mercury off the seat opposite, thumbed to the 'for sale' section, scanned down to the bike ads.

I took another gulp of rum, as I sifted through the different ads, then about halfway down the page there it was, 'Suzuki 125 GPZ, two years old, twenty-four thousand miles on the clock, £350 or nearest offer'.

It sounded absolutely perfect. The perfect age, price and the CC; 125 was the biggest bike I could get as a learner. It would certainly shit all over Tank's Fizzy.

I checked out another couple of ads, then thumbed to the news. It was the usual whiny, panic-inducing bullshit, so I tossed it aside and sat back again, swigging the rum as the scenery scrolled past the window.

Cambridge station came into view, so I quickly ripped the ads page from the newspaper, standing up ready to alight. As we slowed at the station, I swayed sideways, grabbing the seat to steady myself. I thought, whoa, I'm not pissed, already, am I? Nah surely not. It didn't feel like I was. I just felt warm inside, comfortable, chilled out.

The quintessential rum buzz, but when I brought the bottle up to my eye, I saw there was only about a quarter of it left.

Snorting to myself, I hid the bottle, got off the train, and fell into line with the other passengers walking up towards the automated barriers.

In front of me, a goth girl about my age fed her ticket into the barrier. It spat back out of the top, the gate opened, and she walked through with me tight in behind her. She stopped abruptly, scrutinising me.

"Sorry, the service is diabolical, I'm not paying for this shit," I told her, with a grin plastered on my face.

Her face broke into a pleasant smile. "Too right," she replied, pumping her fist.

I smiled, pumped mine back, turned left out of the station as she did, and we awkwardly fell into step next to each other.

The Junction was just around the corner from the station, so I ventured. "Er... You going to see Savage Circle?"

She smiled broadly. "Yes, I am, they're brilliant, are you going?"

I nodded back, thinking, here we go again, another Savage fucking Circle fan.

"Have you heard the new single, 'Over Idiot Educated?'" she asked.

Internally I deflated, thinking, yes, yes, of course bloody I have, and if I told you how I heard it you wouldn't believe me.

"Are you alright?" she probed.

"Yeah... I er, I've just drunk half a bottle of rum," I said, pulling open my jacket,

"Well, most of it."

She laughed. "Brilliant! It's expensive in Cambridge, isn't it? My mate Mia's going to sneak a bottle of voddy into the gig, we're going to get wasted."

I came to a halt. "Mia?"

"Yes, do you know her?" she queried.

"Not really, I met her in the Greenman."

She chortled, "It's a small world, isn't it?"

Nodding, I thought, yeah, it's fucking tiny.

"You must know Sulli and Ray and Tezz and of course Savy; he's a brilliant guitarist."

"Naahhh, never heard of them, I was only there once. Look, I just need to make a phone call, I'll probably see you there."

"Oh, OK. By the way, I'm Cynthia or Sin for short."

"Dean, Dean Reynolds."

"OK Dean… I'll see you later. Oh, and if you haven't got a ticket, you better look lively, because they've almost sold out, and you won't be able to use my ticket again," she laughed.

I creased a smile. "Cheers Sin, bye," I waved, watching her striding off in her high-heeled purple boots.

Once she was out of sight, I sat down on a low wall, watching the lights of Cambridge flicker on, and again I started having my doubts about being here. This was their home turf, and everyone seemed to love them. Talk about surrounded and outgunned. I had just met a total stranger getting off the train who knew them. I wondered if I was to randomly approach someone else, would they know them too? It was ridiculous, even if Renny showed up, it would still be two against, God knows how many.

It's time to go home, I thought, but first, it's time for rum.

Rum sealed up my punctured confidence, and I ventured on to the gig, to find I was right, everyone did love them. The queue was all around the venue.

Taking another gulp of Rum, head down, I began making my way past the line of assembled punks, metal heads and goths.

"Skinner?"

My head shot up.

Hermit John was standing there, looking animated. "Thought that was you." He gestured with his hand. "Here, cut in."

"Cheers John, appreciate it... How are you mate?" I enquired, edging a goth backwards. "Haven't seen you since the Greenman."

"Oh, yeahhh man, that was a crazy good night."

"Can't believe you're out and about again. That's twice in two years," I joked.

Hermit John scratched his chin, puzzled, doing the maths. "Three times. I had to go to my grandmother's funeral."

I wasn't sure whether to laugh or not, so I just nodded thoughtfully.

"I don't like punk rock," he continued. "For me, it's just a racket, but Savage Circle are awesome, incredibly good, amazingly talented people."

You would have thought I'd be used to hearing that by now, but I wasn't. In fact, the more I heard the worse it got.

"Have you heard the new single, 'Over Idiot Educated'?" he asked, animatedly.

I reached for my bottle, drank the last shot and looped it over my shoulder towards the busy road. There was a distant crash, a screeching of tyres, then someone shouted, 'Oi!'

Hermit John gawped at me. "Right... I-I think I need to make a phone call; I'll see you later Skinner."

"Fucking punks," raged the driver, and sped off.

Fuck this, I thought, I'm not waiting here any longer, it's time for some action.

I strutted up to the front of the queue and told the young bloke in the ticket office that my name was Dean Reynolds, and that I had a package for Savy's girlfriend, Mia that she wanted as soon as possible.

He stuttered out some bullshit I couldn't hear, then after checking the guest list many times, he checked the general sales, found the name, and waved me in.

Nice one, I thought, I'm not paying to see these wankers after all, Renny can stump up the readies, he took a cut from that sword.

I smiled at the unintended joke, strolling into the main arena to find Savage Circle were already taking to the stage while the tightly packed crowd were going mad.

Sulli drew his mic up, grinning. "Good evening, we are Savage Circle... Weyyy..." he shielded his eyes to look at the crowd. "So many familiar faces."

"Wanker, fucking wanker," I shouted, but it was lost in the cheers.

Sulli glanced around at the others, they all gave him a nod and they launched into their first number, sending the place into raptures. The punks and goths around me slammed into each other, jumping about, loving it, while all I wanted to do was fuck the place up, ruin it for everyone.

I thought, fuck this for a game of soldiers, I need a piss, so I rammed my way through the euphoric crowd, booted the bog door open and went in.

Once the spring door had snapped shut, it became surprisingly quiet inside.

Still full of anger, I went into one of the traps, had a piss and started splashing it all over the place. I thought about how those bastards had almost made me homeless; how they could still make me homeless.

The red mist took over. I kicked the solid wood toilet seat from its housings sending it clattering to the floor, then stamped on it, trying to smash it to bits. It cracked but didn't break, so I snatched it up, ran back into the main arena and chucked it with everything I had. It hurtled across the polished wood floor like a rogue curling stone, ricocheting off people's boots.

From behind me, hands fell onto my shoulders.

I balled my fists, ready, ready for anything, turned. It was Mia. She was shouting something. She pushed me backwards and we both fell into the ladies toilets.

"Fucking hell Skinner what are you doing?"

"I'm just showing my appreciation for the band."

She scrutinised me for what felt like a very long time, then she creased up laughing. "You haven't changed much, have you?"'

"No nor have you, you're still fucking beautiful, come here," I said, pulling her towards me.

I felt a slight resistance, then she was kissing me back, pushing her tongue into my mouth, her arms pulling me into her.

Responding, I rubbed my hands furiously up and down her thighs.

"Why now?" she asked, fervently.

"I'm on my own now... It's my one big regret in life, that I didn't go back to yours after the Greenman. That, and never seeing the Sex Pistols play.

Mia cracked up. "Yeah, mine too, come on let's put that right. I want you to fuck me, fuck me right now."

She pushed me into one of the traps, kissing me hard. Then she undid my belt, ripped down my jeans and boxers and my cock bounced up. She took it in her hand and started wanking me off. I groaned, threw my head back and put my hand on her shoulder to guide her downwards. She laughed, shook her head, turned, bent over the toilet, lifted her skirt up and tugged her knickers down.

I pulled her perfect arse cheeks apart found her wet cunt and eased myself into her. She gasped, pushing her arse up, and rammed backwards.

I cupped her full breasts, while she put her hands on my arse and we went at it, our moans echoing around the tiled walls.

A few minutes later we were still going at it when the door to the arena opened.

Sound rushed in, then as the door shut it fell silent again.

"Mia?"

I slowed my pace.

"Miaaaa, are you in there?" the voice sang.

"Er, hi Sin," she said, breathlessly.

"Are you OK?"

Mia said, "Yeah, I'm fine," meaning every word of it.

"I just wanted to warn you, that knob head Skinner's here."

I picked up my pace again. So did Mia.

"Oorwh is he? I'll keep a loook out for hiiiim."

Sin was quiet for a moment, then she said, "Right… I'll see you in a minute."

Savage Circle's music blasted in, then it was gone.

Mia and me cracked up laughing, then she smacked me hard on the thigh and we got back to it.

People talk about brewer's droop and other associated erectile dysfunctional problems after a drink, and I must admit I'd had a couple of problems in the past but not tonight. When I came, I came with my whole body.

It was like every pore on my body came. It was incredible, mind-blowing, body-blowing. Whether it was because she was Savy's girlfriend, or that the sex was the purest form of filth I'd had in a long time, or just that she was cool, witty, insightful, and incredibly beautiful, I didn't know.

One thing I did know was that the chaos was just beginning for Mr. Jimmy fucking Saville and his band Savage Circle. It was time to fuck up the gig now.

As I made my way to the outside door Mia grabbed me.

"Listen you need to leave now, there's a lot of people here who want to hurt you."

"Sorry Mia, I can't do that," I told her, looking deep into her.

"Why Skinner?" she insisted, stepping in front of me, blocking the way.

"Because I've got to finish this."

"What, because a man's got to do what a man's got to do?" she rolled her eyes.

"Oh, leave it out Mia, you don't know what you're talking about. Your wanker of a boyfriend Savy and his mates have been down my place saying that I'm dead the next time they see me. One way or another, it ends tonight."

"OK, have it your own way, but there's four of them in the band, and their mate Tezz is one of the bouncers. He's about six feet tall… You know him, don't you?"

"No."

"The one who drives the Cabstar?" she retorted.

"What's a Cabstar?"

"Oh do fuck off Skinner, you nicked his cannabis plants."

I shrugged my shoulders. "So fucking what?"

"Bye, bye, Skinner," she said, condescendingly, moving aside.

"See you Mia, take care of yourself," I returned, sarcastically.

Savage Circle's reworking of the Sickos track 'When the Snake Bit the Sun' hit me square in the face as I bundled through the door. The place was absolutely jumping.

No wonder. It was a great track. My head nodded while I dodged my way through the scrum of sweaty bodies towards the front.

Once I had made it, I wiped the rivulets of sweat off my forehead, then leant onto the stage and took in the band.

Sulli was centre stage, spitting venom into the mic, while Savy was off to the other side of the stage, laying down the glorious bar chords.

For some reason, he was wearing an Angus Young schoolboy's cap. What a wanker, I thought.

Sulli sprung over to my side of the stage, dropped down on his knees and bellowed, "Eating ourselves alive, we're eating ourselves alive, no hope, just dope, we'll never survive."

As he passed the mic into the heaving mass, I snapped it out of his hand.

"You fucking wankers, wankers, fucking wankers," I bawled.

Sulli's eyes almost popped out of his head. He made a grab for his mic, he was too slow. I shouted again and he kicked me square in the face.

I hardly felt it, just kept on shouting into the mic, "You fucking posh wankers, wankers wan-"

The mic went dead, so I dropped it into the mass of boots, hauled myself up onto the stage and legged it. Shoulder barging Sulli out of the way, I ran at Savy.

He put his guitar up like a lance, I elbowed it out of the way, snatched his pathetic cap and dived back into the crowd.

People around me were creasing up laughing as I waved the cap above my head, sticking up two fingers at the band who had now stopped playing.

Then from out of the wings the silhouette of a tall bloke appeared. He dropped down into the crowd, who instantly parted. He raised his right arm and something solid smashed down on my head, sending me sprawling to the floor.

Time stopped. I must've blacked out.

When I came to, Renny's worried-looking face was in my face. His lips moved but I couldn't hear anything apart from a dull monotonous ringing.

Slowly, I began to make out the odd word. Cunts, fuck, and fucking arseholes were the first ones. Then the ringing switched to a high-pitched whine and my head started throbbing horribly.

I rubbed at my aching head. It felt wet. Looking at my hand, I saw blood. A lot of it. I slid my fingers back through my hair. It was saturated in blood.

Unsteadily, using Renny as a crutch, I rose up.

Once I was up, I started shouting but no one could hear me though.

The band had started playing again.

Crisscrossing the stage, the lights passed over me, and I began to see how much blood there actually was. I was covered in it. The front of my T-shirt was soaked, my jeans too, and when I leant forward it was streaming into my eyes.

Renny shouted, "Fucking hell Skinner, you look like a jam rag," in my ear, then, when he saw I wasn't laughing, he changed tack. "Don't worry mate, we're going to sort these bastards out once and for all. I'm calling Robbo."

I slowly shook my head. "No, I want a one-on-one with the cunt who smacked me."

Renny frowned. "That's not a good idea, that looks bad, you might need stitches in that, you might be concussed," he said loudly, turning to Carrie.

Carrie gently put her hand on my head. I flinched, jerking away. She stood back, giving Renny a little nod.

"We should get you to A&E mate."

"What is she a nurse?" I called out over the music.

"Yeah, she is, a veterinarian nurse, that's better for you," he joked.

I snorted. "Nah… I'm not going anywhere mate, seriously."

Renny scraped his hand down his face. "OK, it's up to you."

Savage Circle finished their set and didn't bother to leave the stage before starting the first of their encore tracks. It looked like they were in a hurry - like they had something else on their minds. I thought, good, I'm getting through, I'm fucking your gig up and there's plenty more to come you bastards.

During, 'Jesus Saves at the NatWest' from out of the mad crowd, Sin appeared, her eyes narrowed. "Dean Reynolds? Wanker!" she shrieked at me.

Carrie must have heard it totally differently; she must have thought Sin was having a go at Renny because she marched forward and smacked Sin around the face with her palm. Shocked, Sin staggered backwards, then retaliated by running at Carrie, grabbing her hair and they both fell into a heap on the floor.

A few moments later the tall bouncer appeared. He bent his lofty frame down, snatched Carrie's arm and pulled violently, trying to separate the girls.

Renny was straight on him, grabbing him by the throat, thrusting him backwards into a throng of pogoing punks.

It wasn't funny, but I couldn't help grinning seeing Renny, who was about five-foot-eight, staring up, threatening this six-foot-two bouncer.

The lanky bouncer flailed back this way and that, like a fish on a hook, trying to push Renny off, but he couldn't break the vice-like grip.

Renny pulled him in close and began yelling into his ear, pointing at me. Lanky looked over and nodded. Renny let him go and he elbowed his way back into the crowd.

He sidled up next to me. "He says he'll see you out the back when the band's finished."

I nodded, then looked down. The girls were still rolling around on the floor.

Renny smiled broadly. "You were right about having a girlfriend Skinner," he smiled.

Rubbing at the rapidly growing lump on the top of my head, I watched as they both clambered up, then Carrie propelled Sin back into the riving wall of punks.

"Carrie's great, isn't she? She's my best mate. She's my best mate and she's got nice tits and a nice arse, what more could you ask for?" he enthused, opening his arms to his returning hero.

Renny cuddled his best mate, and they shared a kiss. Then he took a twenty-pound note out of his pocket and handed it to her for the train fare, indicating that it was time for us to go.

Back on stage, Sulli announced their last number 'Spit in the Sky' to the flagging yet still enthusiastic crowd, while we took the opportunity to get out of the arena before the whole place blew up again.

Renny and me pressed our way back through the mass of sweat-encrusted bodies into the foyer, where Renny paused by the ticket office and pointed at the bloke behind the counter.

"Wanker," he stated.

I stifled a laugh, thinking, I know what that's about.

Once we were out of the Junction I took the lead, made my way around the back, thinking, it was easy enough smacking some bloated virgin over the head with a rolling pin back on the Farm, easy enough bringing a brick of fifties back from Lambeth. No problem. I just did it, hadn't given it a second thought. That's how I needed to be now. It was the only way. If I kicked the shit out of this lanky twat, Tezz, or whatever his name was, it would send a message to Savy not to mess with me anymore. I'd had enough of their bullshit.

It was time to hurt someone, hurt someone badly.

In the orange glow of the Junction's car park, Renny and me strutted, keeping our eyes peeled for any wankers hiding behind the rows of cars. I stopped and pointed.

Next to the stage door, there was a Cabstar double-parked, with a minibus alongside it.

Renny gave me a nod, and we strolled over to have a look.

On the back window of the minibus, somebody had stuck a card with, 'If it ain't Savage it ain't worth a fuck' written on it.

I snorted, slowly traced my finger across the card, moved around to the side and looked at Renny.

"Listen, the music's stopped," he said.

He was right, all we could hear now was the traffic on the surrounding roads.

"You sure you're up for this Skinner? Your head looks bad."

"I'm fine mate," I said, not giving a fuck if I was or not.

Sounds of an incoming train built up on the track behind us.

"Listen, Skinner, we don't have to do this. We can wait till they come down the Farm again and batter them."

Shrieks of laughter and joyful shouts reverberated around the building as people left the gig.

"Nah seriously, I can handle this," I assured him, picking up a discarded lemonade bottle.

I smashed it onto a kerb stone, hoping to make a weapon out of it, but ended up with just the lid in my hand.

Quickly dropping it, I moved over to the wall by the stage door and leant on it, waiting for the lanky twat to show.

The train wailed by, shaking the ground beneath us.

The wall behind me fell away, so I put my hands out to balance myself. Then I realised it hadn't moved.

I shook my head, trying to work out what happened, then gently placing my fingers on the lump on my head, a lightning bolt of pain split my head in two.

"Arrrhhh, fucking hell!" I spat.

"Come on Skinner, this is bullshit, we're going," Renny demanded.

"You fucking go, I'm going nowhere."

Renny shook his head. "Fucking Skinner… Look, it's been ten minutes now, they've bottled it, mate. Come on. Let's go."

"I'm not going, man."

Another train pulled into the station, then headed out.

"Oh well, that's Carrie gone now. Cheers, I'll be sleeping at my nan's tonight rather than with her."

"OK, OK, let's fucking go," I said, standing up with a house brick in my hand.

Before Renny could say anything, I lobbed it through the Cabstar's front window.

Renny was stunned, then he bent over, fumbling in the dark, then stood back up with a brick.

"Here Skinner, there's plenty more here," he said, then hurled his straight through the side window of the bus.

I cracked up, legged it over to him, grabbed a couple more myself, then started chucking them, rapid-fire. Glass was flying all over the place. It wasn't enough for Renny, though, he jumped onto the flat back of the Cabstar, kicked the back window in and started pissing into the cab.

Renny smirked. "That's the most useful thing that's going to do tonight." He zipped up quickly, jumped down and started to walk. "Come on let's get out of here before they call the old bill."

A couple more throws and I moved into step next to him.

I chuckled, pulling a piece of card from my pocket. "Check this out," I told him. "'If it ain't Savage it ain't worth a fuck,'" I read, cracking up.

Renny snorted. "That Cabstar ain't worth a fuck now."

Chapter Fourteen

No Sleep 'til Hertford

In the early hours of the next morning, I jolted awake. I didn't feel right; I felt bloated, queasy, disorientated. I sat myself up, took a deep breath and stretched my arms out trying to alleviate the pressure in my stomach, but it just carried on building up. I took another deep breath and dry heaved into my hand.

I knew what was coming, so I clamped my mouth shut, bolting for the toilet.

By the time I'd got my head over the bowl my nose was dripping snot and my mouth was full of sick. Opening my mouth wide, I watched last night's rum and chips cascade into the water below. Feeling a bit better now, I let out a sigh of relief, then stood up to wash my mouth out at the sink.

Once I had got all the gunk out of my mouth, I checked my reflection in the bathroom mirror. Dark lines under red eyes, I looked my normal self. Then dropping my head forward, I examined the lump.

It hadn't bled any more since I had cleaned it the night before, there was just a thin red water-like substance on the scab. Giving it a gentle prod with my forefinger, it was a little sore but OK, considering what I had felt at the time.

From off the top of the cistern, I picked up Savy's Angus Young schoolboy cap, then dropped it on my head.

One glance in the mirror told me, yeah, that's alright for the Aussie rocker, it's part of his stage act, but I look like a right fucking bellend. I suppressed a laugh, shaking my head thinking, that night was fucking hilarious.

Chucking the cap in the swing bin, I strolled downstairs to get some breakfast.

The TV was blasting out from the sitting room, so I barged in, saw Pete, spliff in hand, watching Breakfast Time.

"Wake and bake Skinner?" he smiled, offering me the pungent stick.

"Nah, you're OK mate, I've got work."

Pete withdrew his offer, plugging the spliff back into his mouth, "Ah yes work, I remember that…" he told me through plumes of sweet white smoke.

"Bollocks you do, you're a student."

Pete burst into laughter. "Who's doing the honours today, or is it me?"

"Stay where you are, you lazy sod, I'll sort it," I said, heading for the kitchen.

While the kettle boiled, I snatched up four pieces of bread, dealing them like cards under the grill.

Returning to the sitting room I said, "You know my boss, Hugh? He told me I'm on special duties today, whatever that means."

"Why? Because you sabotaged the tractor?"

I fell about laughing. "Nah, that's all blown over now… You know Lord Laing thought it was his fault for not getting it serviced properly. He actually apologised to Hugh, what a tit eh?"

Pete puffed out another white plume, chortling. "Bloody hell," he said, stubbing out the spliff, then he fell silent, zoning out to the glare of the TV.

Chuckling to myself, I thought, you're a one spliff Cliff, mate then I switched my attention to the bullshit on TV too.

Frank Bough was going on about the dangers of drug use again. It was surprising, his level of knowledge was impressive. He really knew what he was talking about.

I sniffed the air, then sniffed again. There was a smell of smoke in the room, not weed smoke either, something acrid and noxious.

The fire alarm went off. Pete's eyes pinged open wide and he choked, jerking forward, going into a full-blown coughing fit.

"Fucking hell, the house really is on fire," he croaked, then doubled over, coughing his guts up.

Oh shit, the toast, I thought, running for the kitchen. I opened the door to the hall, and it was full of thick black smoke. In the kitchen it was even worse, the four pieces of bread I had put under the grill weren't just burnt, they were on fire.

I pulled the smoking tray out, it was red hot, I shouted,

Aarrrhhh fucking hell," and the whole lot clattered onto the lino.

Sliding on an oven glove, I began plucking the slices of blazing bread up one by one like I was some kind of a wading bird catching a fish. I grabbed the tray and chucked the whole lot into the sink and threw the taps on.

The fire alarm was still trilling away. It was making my head hurt, so I ripped it off the wall, stamping on it until it was silent.

Back in the sitting room, Pete was still coughing his guts up.

"Sorry about that Pete, toasts off mate. I'll get us both a nice cup of tea, how does that sound?" I shouted, throwing the kitchen windows open.

"OK, Skinner... Milk, no sugar," he wheezed back.

I made him a cup of tea, then wandered back through the smoke-engulfed hall, gently sipping it. My mouth had been dry when I'd woken up this morning, but now, after cremating the bread, I was parched.

Pete had opened the patio door, and all windows in the sitting room, made his way out to the patio where he was bent over, hacking away.

I pulled the net curtain aside, went outside, took another sip of the tea and he looked up and put his hand out.

"Is that mine?" he asked.

"Er yeah," I said, handing it to him.

He took a sip. "Ahh. No milk and lots of sugar, just how I like it," he said, sarcastically. "No wonder you don't wake and bake, you're still going from last night." he joked.

I laughed. "I'm sorry Pete, I don't know where my heads at today. Look, I'd better go... Janine's coming back tomorrow, isn't she?"

Pete's face aged about thirty years. "Yeah," he said, defensively.

"Don't worry man, I'll give you a hand cleaning the place up when I get back, OK?"

"Cheers Skinner, good man."

I strolled back through the sitting room, carefully avoiding the piles of encrusted plates, cups and discarded take-away containers, thinking, it doesn't take long for things to get out of hand, but a couple of hours tidying tonight, and we'll have this place ship shape and shiny for the commandant's return.

Absently scratching at the lump on my head, I sauntered out to the van, hopped in, and got underway.

Hugh had asked me to meet him at the annexe around eight o'clock. It was only half seven, and with the annexe only a fifteen-minute drive away from the Farm.

I would be on time for once. It was only right. Hugh was alright really, even though he was suspicious about the mechanical failures at Hunsdon House, he had stuck up for us. We'd been back onsite the next day and I swore I saw him looking over at the cut-up croquet lawn, chuckling to himself. I wonder what these special duties are, I thought, as I parked up behind his Volvo in the alley next to the annexe.

Crossy and Hugh emerged from the annexe straining under heavy wooden boxes.

"Morning Skinner, can you grab one of those tea chests in the foyer? Stick it in the back of my car, please."

"Hi Hugh, yeah, of course mate," I smiled. "Morning Morris," I crowed, at his sidekick.

"That's Mr Cross, or Crossy to you," he returned, belligerently.

"Right you are Morris," I grinned, ducking into the annexe.

There were six tea chests filled to the brim with swords, paintings, boxes of old parchments and coins. It was a proper treasure trove.

Once we had loaded up Hugh's car and Crossy had pissed off, Hugh and me shared a roll-up, while he filled me in on my special duties for the day.

I was to meet him at the dig in Ware, where we'd pick up the generators and water pumps that the unit had been using to drain the site, then we would set off for Peterborough. I would follow him up the A10, then we'd cut across the countryside to Flag Fenn, near Peterborough, then drop off the generators and water pumps to help them out with their waterlogged site. Then we'd carry on to Peterborough Museum and drop off the tea chest treasure trove.

Sounds good to me, I thought. It was only going to take four hours maximum, so we'd be back by two at the latest. Then that would be it. I could go home. It couldn't have worked out any better. I would go back to the Farm, help Pete clear up, get a few zeds then I'd be fresh for another party at Lenny the Lamp's place tonight.

I wanted to be on good form, as Renny had told me that Carrie was bringing her best mate, Alice, another rocker girl, along. Apparently, she'd seen my old band Virus V1 play at Ware College and thought I'd looked alright.

If she's nice, I thought, I hope the place gets raided again, then I can whisk her back to mine for a few spliffs.

"Skinnerrrrrr? Are you OK?" enquired Hugh,

"You seem to be off it, even more than usual."

"Sorry, I'm not my best today. Right, shall I follow you down to Ware?"

Hugh frowned, quickly glanced left then right, "No. No. No, I need to go home and er… Let the dogs out."

I smiled at the bloke. "Thought you didn't like dogs, Hugh?"

"Oh, I don't, Mrs. Borill does. So, yes, I'll meet you down there."

Watching his sagging Volvo rattle off up the cobblestoned alley, I thought, I bet that nice English Civil War Halberd doesn't make it to Peterborough. Oh well, better it's in his home with someone who loves and understands its significance, than collecting dust in some empty old museum.

I snorted, hopped into my van. For a moment I thought I'd lost my footing, as the whole world seemed to sway like I'd hopped into a rowing boat. I shook my head. My ears popped, then I heard an irritating high-pitched whistling sound.

Trying to get rid of it, I frantically pumped my finger in my ear, shook my head again, and thankfully it faded away. Then I started feeling hot, but when I placed my hand on my forehead it was clammy, stone cold. It was weird. I hadn't had a hangover before but from what people had told me, this wasn't part of it.

I sat there for a little while, yawning expansively while sinking into the chair, then I thought, this is ridiculous, if I want to get back by two, I need to go. Go now.

Turning over the engine, I stamped on the accelerator.

In the car park at the back of the Indian restaurant near the Ware dig, I parked up and saw Hippy John in discussion with the manager.

Hippy John waved, and mooched over, "Hey man? Watch out for Tank - he fancies a day out," He looked up and scrutinised my head. "…Oh, wow man, have you been fighting?"

"Nah, I fell mate," I grinned.

"Where from, the Post Office Tower?"

I creased up.

Hippy John smiled, glanced up and grimaced. "Hey Tank," he greeted, as Tank popped up, placing his hands on the door frame, and craning his neck in through the passenger side window.

"OK Skinner, if you back the van over to the crew shed, the pumps and generators are in there - let's get this done before Hugh gets here," he told me, all official-like.

I nodded, started the van, then slowly backed up to the shed, carefully avoiding the other diggers, who were chatting in the early morning sunshine.

Tank tapped on the back of the van when I was in the right spot.

"OK, OK, perfect," he told me.

I switched off the engine, got out, strode around the back, and flung open the doors.

Viv, Astrid, and Muncher brought the first generator out, straining as they heaved it up and into the back.

Tank and me went in for the next one. We lifted it up, waddled over to the van and slid it in next to the other one.

Tank put his thumb up, gave me a big smile and went back inside.

I stood back and watched as Pat and Tank brought the two lightweight water pumps.

Tank grinned, then furrowed his brow. "You look as white as a sheet Skinner."

I smiled broadly. "Yeah, it's a punk rocker's suntan," I laughed. "Nah, I was on the piss last night, drunk half a bottle of rum."

"That would do it," Tank said, laughing.

"Right, let's get this lot anchored in place," I told him.

He smiled ingratiatingly, putting his thumb up again.

Using bungee straps, I hooked them all together, closed the door, locked it, and sat back, waiting for Hugh to arrive.

A few moments later Tank joined me, passing me a lit-up readymade roll-up.

"So, this lot's going up to Peterborough, is it?"

I took a big lung full. "Yep," I said cagily.

"Those generators are heavy aren't they?"

"Yep."

There was a bang on the window. It was Hugh.

"OK, out you come Tank."

"No, Skinner wants me to help him, don't you mate?"

"Nah, not really," I laughed. "You're not qualified."

Hugh cracked up. "Come on Tank, out you come, you're not going. I'm not going to let you two loose in Peterborough Museum. You two seem to cause chaos everywhere you go."

Tank sulkily undid his seat belt, threw open the door and stalked off.

"OK, Skinner, let's go. You won't need a map, just follow me," he instructed, striding over to his Volvo.

Hugh pulled out of the car park, and as I spun the wheel to follow him, I saw Tank sitting despondently, puffing the last of his roll-up.

I pointed to myself. "Qualified," I told him, and he laughed back, showing me two fingers.

I followed Hugh along the A10, down through the rib valley into my old village and up onto High Cross Hill. After that, the hills slowly melted away, then disappeared altogether as we crossed over the county line into Cambridgeshire.

Once we had passed the low grey buildings of Cambridge, the roads became straight and monotonous, the scenery was non-existent. With nothing to look at and nothing much to do except keep the van moving in a straight line, my concentration started to wane, and as my concentration died away the high-pitched whistling I'd heard outside of the annexe returned. Returned with a vengeance.

I swept my hand back over my head, pressing down hard on my scalp, trying to squeeze the noise out, trying to get it to stop. It just wailed, on and on, biting at my already fragile nerves. It then intensified. I flinched, like I had been stung, then pumped my finger in my ear again, trying to rid myself of it. It wouldn't go away.

Fuck it, I thought, grabbing Voivod's 'War and Pain' cassette, I'll drown the bastard out.

Pushing it into the stereo, rough guitars and gruff vocals spewed out.

Immediately the whine rescinded, lost in the maelstrom.

I put my foot down to catch up with Hugh.

In front of us, it was a straight road going all the way to the horizon. Looking in the rear-view mirror, it was exactly the same.

To the sides of us, there were two sweeping irrigation ditches with brick culverts for farm vehicles to cross over.

Suddenly, I felt tired. Very tired.

Hunching over the steering wheel, I tried to focus on the controls, on the rapidly scrolling road, on Hugh's blurred car up ahead. I became lightheaded, out of step with my surroundings, like I was someone else looking through my eyes.

My head nodded forward.

I slapped myself on the cheek, trying to stay awake, trying to concentrate, trying to keep in control. It worked momentarily but my eyelids soon drooped, shut tight and my head smacked down onto the steering wheel. I hauled myself up, slapping myself again, only a lot harder this time, stinging my hand and cheek.

My eyes shut.

I lolled forward, hitting my forehead on the steering wheel.

My eyes opened.

Up ahead, Hugh had slowed to a crawl, his brake lights blinked on, and I watched his number plate getting closer and closer.

I snapped myself out of the haze, slammed the brakes on.

The tyres gripped and I skidded to a stop, a foot from his bumper.

Hugh's eyes appeared in his rear-view mirror, looking at me questioningly.

Pulling a tight smile, I put my hand up.

In front of him, a tractor appeared indicating right and it bounced over one of the brick culverts, leaving deep cuts in the mud.

I thought, fucking hell, what am I going to do? If I get out and tell him, I can't go any further, I need to shut my eyes, it would be embarrassing. And even if he said, OK, what's he going to do? Sit in his fucking motor waiting for me, while I have a mid-morning siesta?

Nah, no way, I'll keep going. Whatever the problem is, it'll go away just like it did after I left the annexe.

Hugh pulled away and I followed, took the van up to about fifty miles an hour, then my head nodded forward again. I heaved it back up with my hand, thinking fuck this, then started biting my hand, forcing the life-confirming pain up my arm.

I was wide awake, took a deep breath, then I was gone.

I came to, with the van listing to one side, racing along the irrigation ditch, totally out of control. Cow parsley shot past my window. Snaps and cracks came from the front as the van ripped through the undergrowth. I kicked down hard on the brakes with both feet. The wheels began to grip. I thought, I'm going to be OK, I'm going to be OK. Then from out of the undergrowth came a wall of bricks.

There was a massive crash. I shot forward and I was out.

**

I tasted blood.

My lips felt puffed up.

I hauled my head up off the steering wheel.

My eyes flicked open.

Scarred orange and red bricks of a culvert.

The bonnet creased upwards like a pyramid.

Then, I saw flames flickering up through the gaps at the front of the bonnet.

Slowly, it crept up around the bonnet towards me. Smoke began to billow out of the stereo.

Panic ripped through me.

I pulled on the door handle. It wouldn't open. I tried again. It was useless, so I began ramming the door with my shoulder, desperately trying to break free.

It wouldn't budge. It was jammed. I was trapped.

The cab filled up with smoke. I couldn't see. Coughing hard, I began to choke.

Reaching for the window crank, I furiously wound it.

It stopped about halfway down.

Pushing myself up with my arms I tried to wriggle through the hole, but it was too narrow, then I remembered the hammer under my seat.

I reached down in the billowing smoke, fumbled, grabbed, fumbled again, finally grabbed it, pulled it up and laid into the glass. It fell away and I threw myself out the window, then hauled myself out of the drainage ditch and up onto the road and

ran and ran until I couldn't run anymore. Out of breath, I turned, saw a tower of smoke, twisting, rising into the clouds and below it, the van engulfed in flames.

I lurched forward, fell, and everything went black.

Other titles by Mick N. Baker

Tales of Angelic Upstarts

Bad Brains Tales

Tales of Disorder

The Tale of the Clash

All available on Amazon, Barnes and Noble and Bookshop.org

Savage Circle

Printed in Great Britain
by Amazon